Grandpa's War:
The World War I Experiences
of Cpl. John G. Rakers

Mark Armato

Grandpa's War:

The World War I Experiences of Cpl. John G. Rakers

CW Book Lady.com Publishing

Independence MO. 64053

2014 Publication

The author, Mark Armato and his beloved grandpa.
Ramsey, Illinois, 1959

Dedication

I'd like to dedicate this work to my four children;
Sammy, Hannah, Vinny, and Joe.
I love you all very much.

Dad

Table of Contents

Foreword   9

Introduction   11

Chapter I

    A Different Time   17

Chapter II

    War   27

Chapter III

    Uncle Sam Raises an Army   34

Chapter IV

    Drafted   39

Chapter V

    The American Expeditionary Force   49

Chapter VI

    Camp Taylor   60

Chapter VII

    Old Hickory   71

Chapter VIII

    Over There   84

Chapter IX

    Training With the British   96

Chapter X

    Life in the Trenches   104

Chapter XI

    War Stories   111

Chapter XII

    The Ypres-Lyes Offensive   117

Chapter XIII

    The Hindenburg Line   129

Chapter XIV

    In the Thick Of It   139

Chapter XV
        Armistice   164
Chapter XVI
        Coming Home   172
Chapter XVII
        After the War   187
Chapter XVIII
        Epilogue   198
Acknowledgments   201
Bibliography   203
About the Author   207

Foreword

Author, Mitchell A. Yockelson

Borrowed Soldiers: Americans under British Command, 1918

Until the publication of *Borrowed Soldiers* little has been written about American soldiers fighting under British command during the First World War. It's a little known fact that two American divisions, the 30th and 27th, were loaned to the British to help them with their operations in Belgium and France throughout the summer and fall of 1918. Both divisions, who made up the II Corps, saw their fair share of bloody fighting at Ypres, Bellicourt, and St. Souplet. It was at Bellicourt, a battle few Americans have ever heard of, that the American II Corps earned immortality when it attacked and broke the formidable Hindenburg Line.

One of those "borrowed soldiers" was Illinois farm boy, Corporal John George Rakers. In *Grandpa's War* Rakers' grandson, Mark Armato, has affectionately and painstakingly written an account of his grandfather's experiences with the 30th Division during those terrible days. Relying on his grandfather's stories, photographs, newspaper accounts, memoirs, letters, and military records Mr. Armato has put together a moving and dramatic story of one man's experience in the Great War. *Grandpa' s War* is a valuable addition to the stories of those long ago forgotten heroes, whose singular experience deserves to be remembered and honored, especially at this time, as we approach the centennial of America's involvement in that war.

Introduction

Full disclosure; I never did like the First World War very much. I was always much more interested in the Civil War than I ever was with the "Great War." Being a fan of uniforms, I found the uniforms of WWI, with those silly helmets, tight coats, and ridiculous puttees unattractive. The American solider looked like a Boy Scout! (Although the French and English did have some pretty cool uniforms, but then again they usually did). And the reasons for fighting it, once you got past the usual explanations of nationalism, arms races, alliances, and so forth, ultimately seemed absurd to me. It seemed to lack a great purpose like that of the Civil War, with its struggle for the Union and the abolition of slavery. Explain it all you want, but I still found myself scratching my head, and wondering what the hell they were fighting for. Plus I always found the war itself difficult to understand. The unfamiliar geography, with its difficult European names and complicated strategies, only served to confuse me.

And then there was the ugliness. It was so damn ugly. I know, all war is ugly, but WWI was different as far as I'm concerned. The trenches, mud, rats, lice, poison gas, flame throwers, and one bloody, grinding slaughter after another took it to another level. Has there ever been a more futile butchery? There was never anything uplifting, or inspirational about it to me, as it all seemed so pointless. Reading the histories and visiting the museums always left me a little confused, disillusioned, and even....vaguely depressed. World War I is a hard war to "enjoy", you might say.

Yet here I am writing a book about it. Why? The reason is simple. My grandfather, John George Rakers, was a veteran of that war. Beyond that I wouldn't care, but he was part of something monumental that helped shape the world even to this day. He was one of millions, who took part in that war, and I am both proud and fascinated by that fact. He wasn't famous. He didn't do anything memorable, as far as the history books are concerned. But he was my grandfather who had wonderful stories to tell, and that's good enough for me. So to fully tell his story, I had to immerse myself in that filthy war.

I guess you could say this project began when I was a small child, and I first heard Grandpa's stories. Actually, when I think about it, I believe it was Grandma, not Grandpa who started it all for me. I have a memory of sitting in our kitchen with Grandma during one of their visits to Kansas City. It must have been the early 60's, and I was maybe six or seven years old. As is usual with distant memories, the details are unclear, but as I recall the television was on in the living room showing an episode of the old *Jackie Gleason Show*. I remember he was performing in a sketch about a WWI flying ace. Even now I can see Gleason looking dashing in his comical, rotund way, with a pencil mustache, leather flight jacket, goggles on his head and a long scarf about his neck. In any case, this must have prompted some kind of discussion with Grandma, because it was at this time she proudly informed me that my grandfather was a veteran of that war, and that he had been in the *"thick of it"* at some mysterious place called the *"Hindenburg Line"*. With that simple conversation the seed was planted.

Over the years that original memory was added to with stories often told around the dinner table. Typically the tales were humorous, and suitable for dinner conversation. In other less formal moments he would tell me slightly grimmer stories, but never too grim. Like most veterans, I think Grandpa was reluctant to tell too much about what he saw or did. If pressed, he could be diplomatic. Once when I was a small boy, the family was in Ramsey, gathered at the dinner table. With the audacity that only a kid can have, I asked him if he ever shot a German soldier. He could've embarrassed, or scolded me for such a question, but he didn't. Instead he simply said, "I figured if I didn't shoot at them, they wouldn't shoot at me." As an adult I know that can't possibly be true, but looking back on it now, I realize it was the perfect answer.

Perhaps because I showed such an interest, and would often

ask questions, he would tell me more than maybe he would have otherwise. He even gave me a souvenir of the war, a German match box cover made out of a German belt buckle, and shell copper. Embossed on the buckle are the words "Got mit uns" or "God with us". Curators today call it an example of "trench art". I called it cool. The early eighties would add additional layers to my memories. As was my habit in those days I travelled to Ramsey to visit my grandparents for a few days after school let out for summer break. One time I went with more of a purpose, and had the good sense to bring a tape recorder from school to interview Grandpa. We sat in the dining room, and he proceeded to tell me some great, new stuff, including what would become one of my favorite stories about the war. When he was done, he got up and went to the hall closet to retrieve an old photograph that was the object of the story, and like the German belt buckle before, he gave it to me to keep.

As I said before, most of Grandpa's stories were humorous and/or grim in nature, but they never revealed any strong emotions on his part. Grandpa pretty much kept his emotions to himself. And that is what makes the summer of 1985 so special. In a story you will read about in a later chapter, I was honored with a experience that to this day can still bring tears to my eyes. All of these experiences built up an accumulation of memories that have been the foundation of this book.

In April of 1988 my grandfather died. There have been few moments in my life that have had such a dramatic impact on me. I remember vividly the loss I felt, still feel in fact. But what hit me so hard was the potential loss of his stories. They were so much a part of my relationship with Grandpa, that I could not imagine a future without him there, telling me another war story. And not only was it the loss of his stories I feared, but the *loss of stories not yet told*! It hurt. Yet, out of my grief, I experienced a sense of clarity I've rarely felt. I knew that the only way to save those stories, was that somebody would have to write them down. And while I knew that nobody could retrieve stories from the grave, maybe somehow, somebody could do the necessary research that would add those coveted details.

Of course, I knew that *somebody* would have to be me.

I suppose a therapist could have some fun with this, but I recall how after Grandpa died, my single minded attempt to find more details to add to his experiences-details I had never thought to ask about before his death. His discharge papers, given to me by my mom, lit the fire. In the months, even years, that followed, I would travel to the World War I National Museum here in Kansas City, the county courthouse in Shelbyville, Ill., and local libraries, searching for any nugget that could somehow round out his stories. Using both primary, and secondary sources, I was able to fill in some of those gaps. Divisional and regimental histories, old newspapers, letters, interviews, photographs- all were found, and used to help me shape Grandpa's stories.

In time, I had done all the research I thought I needed to do and stopped; besides, other more pressing concerns began to take over. I got married in 1989, started a family, bought a house, and became consumed with all the responsibilities that came with it. I told myself that one day, I would take up that work again and write his story, but for now it was time to move on. So I put it all in my files, and the years began to pass.

It took a family reunion in 2005 to give me the jolt I needed to resume my work. And what an appropriate time it would be, too. The family with all its aunts, uncles, and cousins would be together at Ramsey Lake for the first time in years. And it would be Memorial Day, a perfect day to remember and honor our own veteran, Grandpa. It seemed simple enough. I would take that work, write it up, and everyone would be impressed! I figured ten pages or so should do it. So I began.

As I began to write, I slowly came to realize that ten pages was not going to be enough. My ambition grew, and I realized that for his stories to have some real power, I needed to add more context; in other words, I needed to tell the story behind the story. I would need to do more research, and so over the course of the next few years I did just that, adding even more detail than I ever imagined, but always wishing I could add more. Oh, how many times I wished I had Grandpa there to tell me more! It seemed that the more I learned, the more questions I had; questions that only Grandpa could answer. Trust me, dear reader, writing history can be a frustrating business.

But it is finally done. I have done all I can do. I have written this book not only to save my grandfather's stories, but also to share. I have written this with my children, nieces, nephews, and one day, grandchildren in mind. You all never knew my grandfather. I wish you did. So maybe in some small way, this will help you know him. You can be proud of him. He served his country, and went through hell. Like most veterans, he would never call himself a hero, but in "my book" he is.

Chapter I

A Different Time

The Rakers Family circa 1916
Grandpa is in the back row, 2nd from the left.

Situated in the rolling farmland of the Southwest portion of Shelby County, Illinois, sits the small town of Oconee. The township in which it resides in was well watered with numerous creeks such as the Opossum, Otter, and Coal. Stands of woods provided timber, and there was rich prairie soil where a man could make a good living farming the land. The town was laid out in 1854 and the name Oconee was selected from an Indian word meaning "Beautiful Papoose" or "Indian Maiden". Over the years, people settled in Oconee, including a number of German and Dutch Catholic immigrants. Families with names like Hackel,

Lehn, Eckholt, and Werner built their homes and farmed the land. In August 1868 they were joined by another family from Holland, the Rakers.

Not much is known about the early Rakers, and what we do know comes mostly from stories passed down over the generations. Like most Dutch immigrants of the time, they came to America to make better lives for themselves. There are several versions as to what happened, but apparently the patriarch of the family, Gerhardt Herman Rakers, was a poor, landless tailor. The story has it that two of his sons (or brothers, depending on the version) came to America seeking better prospects. They liked what they saw and decided to stay. Reportedly when their mother Anna heard of their decision she determined that the family must leave their home in Nieuw Schoonebecck and join her sons. "We'll go where our sons are!" she is supposedly to have said. So the family sold all of their belongings, and Gerhardt took the gold they made from the sale, and sewed it into the linings of his children's clothing for safe keeping. They made their way to the port city of Bremerhaven, and set sail in late July, 1868 for America.

They entered the country through Baltimore, and bought themselves a train ticket on the Baltimore and Ohio line heading west to St. Louis. It must have been an exciting adventure and a story is told about how whenever the train would slow down as it negotiated a curve, the Rakers boys would jump off the train, and snatch apples from a nearby orchard. After two days of travel they arrived in Pana, Illinois, where they were met by some Dutch settlers who had preceded them. Then they walked south an additional seven miles, and finally arrived in Oconee, their new home. They bought a small house along what is now highway 51, and it is said they were surprised to find that the barn was not attached to the house as was the custom in the old country. In time, additions were made to the house, and it would be in the Rakers family for generations to come.

In the years that followed Gerhardt and Anna prospered as

farmers, and raised their five sons and three daughters. They were determined to raise their children as good Catholics, but the closest priest was in Pana, and he didn't understand German. Gerhardt took action and was responsible for getting priests to Oconee to say Mass. Masses in those days were performed in people's homes with a roughhewn altar made by one of Gerhardt's sons. Eventually Sacred Heart Church was built, and Anna would serve as the first president of the Altar Society.

Gerhardt and Anna's youngest son was Gerhardt Jr. Born in 1856, he was a mere twelve years old when he left his homeland. On October 22nd, 1880, at the age of twenty- four, he became an American citizen along with his father. Both men travelled to Shelbyville, the county seat, to fill out the paperwork, take an oath to support the U.S. Constitution, and renounce their allegiances to their former countries. Interestingly, the two men had to renounce different countries and kings. Gerhardt Sr. was originally from Germany, and renounced his allegiance to Emperor William of Prussia while Gerhardt Jr. renounced his to King William III of Holland. Seven years later on July 5th, 1887 in a ceremony in Pana, Gerhardt Jr. married Mary Wessels, also of Holland. In short order they began to have a family. On May 29^{th,} 1896, a little over a hundred years ago, my grandfather John George Rakers was born. Despite Grandpa's given name we all knew him as George. Supposedly there were two John's in his grade school classroom. To make matters less confusing, his teacher took to calling him George, and the name stuck.

Grandpa was born into a large family. He was the fifth child and third son of Gerhardt and Mary. All told, his parents would have eleven children, but only eight would survive into adulthood. This was not uncommon in those days, as large families were needed to help on the farm, and with medical science being what it was, infant mortality was high. Of the surviving children Grandpa had three sisters and four brothers. His sister Margaret was the oldest followed by brother Henricus (Henry), then Joannnes Gerhardus (Grandpa), Gerhardus Herman

(Herman), Alphonse, Anna, Leo, and Agnes. Their names reflected their Dutch heritage, and it was common to hear Dutch spoken in the home while growing up. They were a close family who worked hard and went to Sacred Heart Church every Sunday. Here Grandpa would frequently serve as an altar boy.

It was a different world in 1896 when Grandpa was born. The nineteenth century was about to end, and a new way of life was beginning to emerge. So many things which we take for granted today either didn't exist, or were in their infancy. Television and computers of course did not yet exist. The radio was ten years into the future. The telephone was only twenty years old, and most people didn't have one yet. The light bulb was seventeen years old, and the movies were a mere three years old by Grandpa's birth. Man had not yet learned how to fly, and the Wright brothers would not make their historic flight until seven years later in 1903. Electricity? Indoor plumbing? Central heating and cooling? Forget it!

Grover Cleveland was president, serving his second non-consecutive term when Grandpa was born. He was the first Democrat elected president after twenty four years of Republican rule. There had been a depression during Cleveland's second term, and he wasn't very popular with the workers or farmers. In 1896 when Grandpa was six months old, another presidential election took place, and the people voted Cleveland out and restored Republican rule with the election of William McKinley. The economy improved, and the farmers enjoyed good times again.

America was not yet a world power. We consisted of forty-five states (Utah being the 45th), and we had no overseas possessions or territories. There was no United Nations or N.A.T.O., or any such thing. With the exception of some interventions into Latin America, the United States was pretty much uninvolved in foreign affairs. However, that would soon change in 1898, when Grandpa was two years old. We fought the Spanish –American War, became an imperial power, and never looked back.

In 1896 the Civil War had been over for thirty- one years and reconstruction had been over for only nineteen. There were still plenty of Civil War veterans in Shelby County, and most would've been in their fifties in Grandpa's day. It would not have been uncommon to see them in parades, and other patriotic events much like Grandpa would take part in many years later.

In 1896 the population of the United States was roughly 76 million people. America was still mostly rural and agricultural, but that was rapidly changing as industrialization was making us more into city dwellers and factory workers. There were few paved or "hard roads", as folks used to say in those days, and the Illinois Central Railroad was an important transportation link in the region. People still got around by horse and buggy. Grandpa and his brothers could each drive a team of horses. Aunt Agnes, Grandpa's youngest sister, remembered her family going to church with her parents' driving a two wheeled, horse drawn buggy while the rest would walk. Interestingly enough, 1896 was the same year Henry Ford built his first automobile and drove it through the streets of Detroit. Transportation being what it was, the Rakers probably didn't get off the farm very much. The nearest towns were Pana, seven miles north, Ramsey, ten miles south, and Vandalia a further thirteen miles south. Trips would have been infrequent, and no doubt an occasion for excitement, such as the time the whole family put on their Sunday best and went by train to Pana to have a family portrait taken.

People made their own entertainment in those days too. People would talk, play cards, sing, read, socialize, and play games. Professional baseball had been around since 1869, a mere twenty seven years. The National League was formed in 1876, and the American League in 1900. There were teams in St. Louis and Chicago in Grandpa's day, and folks could follow their team's progress, or lack of it, in the newspapers. Speaking of newspapers, Shelby County had thirteen newspapers and it is said that Gerhardt loved to read the paper front to back. He read the

Decatur paper which was delivered by train, and could be picked up at the post office. It was said of him that he was well informed, and could talk knowledgeably about world events. Later in life illness deprived him of this simple pleasure. Missing it desperately, he would have someone read it to him.

Besides baseball, the Rakers may have also been horse racing fans. The same year Grandpa was born, a colt came into this world in Oxford, Indiana. He was a mahogany standard- bred pacer, and his name was Dan Patch. He made his racing debut at the age of four, and ran an impressive two minute, sixteen second mile. By 1903 Dan managed to shave twenty seconds off his time. He came close to a world record in 1904, and one year later he set that record at the Minnesota State Fair before 93,000 screaming fans. His record of one minute, 55 seconds made Dan Patch legendary, and a household name, not to mention a merchandising monster! Even a small nine year- old boy in Oconee heard of him, and was deeply impressed. Grandpa would later draw Dan Patch's picture inside the barn where it stayed for the next century, until a relative cut it out to have it framed.

Just like today weddings, baptisms, and funerals,

would've been a cause for people to gather and take a break from their never ending labor, and relax a bit. People played their own music in those days too. It was the tail end of an era just before the phonograph made an impact on popular culture. It was an era when people still sang in their homes, and the music published in those days was for that purpose. Songs like "A Bicycle Built for Two", "Home on the Range", and "Buffalo Gals" were popular standards of the day. Many families had someone who could play an instrument like a piano or guitar. Just look at any old Sears and Roebuck catalogue from the turn of the century, and you will see an amazing assortment of pianos, mandolins, banjos, horns, violins, guitars, harmonicas, and accordions for sale. Somebody was buying them! The Rakers had a pump organ in the home, and Gerhardt could play it, in fact he was the church organist. Grandpa grew up learning how to play the harmonica and the accordion, the latter supposedly taught to him by his father. Gerhardt loved to wake his children on Christmas morning by playing Christmas carols on the accordion, something Grandpa would do many years later for his own children. Apparently Grandpa was good enough that he would play for barn dances and beer parties that were popular after threshing time. I have many fond memories of listening to Grandpa play tunes such as "Dem Golden Slippers", "Red Wing", "My Country tis of thee", and of course "Red River Valley" In fact many years later my mother taught me how to play that same tune on Grandpa's old Hohner accordion. He gave it to mom after he bought a new one in Germany, and she in turn later gave it to me. Today it is one of my most prized possessions.

Like all families today and long ago, the Rakers followed a predicable routine. They arose early each day before sunrise (Grandpa always did until his dying day) to work on the farm. The day would start with Mary and the girls making breakfast of corn bread or pancakes, or eggs and bacon. In the fall there would be cured ham. After breakfast there would be numerous chores to complete before they'd hit the fields or go to school, as the case may be. Grandpa would go as far as the seventh grade before dropping out of school altogether. The Rakers had ten head of horses, and they had to be curried each day. The barn would have to be cleaned, and the cows milked. Grandpa said he would often fall asleep while milking. Then it was to the fields. They would work throughout the day doing whatever was required for that particular season. Aunt Agnes remembered that the girls would spend the day baking eight to ten loaves of bread a day, as well as cleaning house, tending to the garden, and canning. There were five boys to feed as well as two to three hired hands, and they would get mighty hungry. The girls would bring them lunch in the fields, but in the evening the boys would come home for dinner. At times they would have to work until dark, and on those occasions dinner would be brought to them in the fields. Typical meals consisted of chicken soup, salmon loaves (you could buy canned salmon in Oconee in those days, believe it or not) sausages, ham, beef, vegetables, potatoes, and desserts like cake, pies, and cookies. When the day was done, the boys would go home and no doubt collapse exhausted in the two bedrooms that they shared.

Spring would be planting time. Farming with horses, the Rakers would plant corn and oats. When the corn was as high as your head, Grandpa and his brothers would have to walk the rows of corn and chop weeds. Hot, hard work I'm sure, and probably very boring. However Grandpa and his brothers found a way to lighten things up a bit. They would bring a deck of cards, and when they finished weeding one row, they would sit and play a hand of pitch. Then they would weed another row, and sit and play another hand, and so on. Who knows what Gerhardt thought about that, if he knew about it at all? Chewing tobacco was another way Grandpa passed the time in the fields. Though it must have been frowned upon by his parents. Grandpa once confessed to me that he would often stash a plug on a fence rail in the fields, hiding it, no doubt. That could be risky though, as one time he went out to retrieve it after a rain, only to find that his tobacco was ruined!

In the summer there would be threshing and putting up hay. Fall would be harvest time where they would bale hay and straw, but the big event of the season was the butchering. They would butcher four big hogs and one beef. The hog would be shot, and stuck to bleed it dry. Then they would hang it by its hind feet to scrape the hide. Gerhardt would cut the hog down the center and gut it. Once done, it was time to cut it up, with Gerhardt being very particular about doing it just so. Next they would salt it, and let it lay for several weeks before they would hang it in the smoke house. There was an old stove inside, and Gerhardt would burn hickory wood to produce a lot of smoke. The smoke would waft out of the eaves, and fill the yard with its wonderful smell, a memory Grandpa fondly recalled. The beef wasn't smoked of course, but was soaked instead in a solution of salt brine to preserve it. Once the meat had been properly smoked, the family would grind the pork and make sausages. This would give them all the meat they would need to get through the year.

The fall chores would be followed by winter, but the work didn't stop. Grandpa said they would put in winter wheat, and the boys would also cut ice from a nearby water source. The ice provided the refrigeration needed to preserve their food through the year, and I imagine that Gerhardt, being the entrepreneur that he was, made a little profit selling it too. Winter was also a time to shuck corn. Grandpa said sometimes they would get behind in their shucking, and his father would keep him home from school to help. Grandpa didn't mind though, as he said he'd rather shuck corn than go to school anyway.

And so it went, season after season, year after year. Grandpa quickly grew up, and knew well the rhythms of life on a farm. Life was predictable and routine, with the outside world affecting them very little, if at all. August of 1914 marked the Raker's forty- sixth anniversary of their new life in America. They had done well, and America had fulfilled its promise to them. They enjoyed a prosperity they could've only dreamed of back in Holland. The problems and struggles of the old world were far away, and with the passage of time, slipped further and further from memory. However, the old world wasn't done with the Rakers yet, or with the rest of America for that matter. For despite the separation of an ocean, events in Europe would reach into the homes of America, and pull her sons across the sea, and into the vortex of European politics. So I have to wonder, did the Rakers realize, that summer of 1914, that the murder of an obscure Austrian royal would one day reach across the Atlantic, and threaten their world? What did Gerhardt think as he read about the assassination of the Archduke Francis Ferdinand in his Decatur newspaper?

Three years later in the spring of 1917, Grandpa was twenty-one years old. He stood five feet, nine and a half inches tall. He cut a handsome appearance with his grey eyes, brown hair and fair complexion. He was healthy, and farm work had made him strong and tough. That spring would be like all the other springs he had known. There would be chores to do, and a crop of corn to put in the ground. He had a birthday coming up (although the Raker's didn't celebrate birthdays) and soon he would be twenty-one. Certainly he was thinking about his future. There was also a wedding coming up, as his sister Margaret was to be wed on May 10th. There was much to look forward to. But this spring would be different. War clouds were blowing in from the east like a double header on the Illinois Central. America, the new world, in spite of herself, would soon be asked to save Europe, the old world, from itself. Another generation of Americans' would be called upon to once again make terrible sacrifices for the country. The safe, predicable world the Rakers had known for so long was about to be turned upside down. They didn't know it yet, but John George Rakers was about to go to war.

Chapter II

War!

Newspapers like the New York Times announced to the country
that we were at war!

The purpose of this chapter is to give the reader a brief summary of the events, and causes that led to America's involvement in World War I. To make Grandpa's story more meaningful I think the reader needs to know something about why we were fighting in the first place. It is by no means comprehensive. If the reader wishes to know more about the causes of the war, he or she would be advised to go to the library whose shelves will be stocked with plenty of books that can tell you more.

On the night of April 2nd, 1917, a determined President Woodrow Wilson went before a joint session of congress with a heavy heart. As he walked into the house chamber, its members erupted in deafening applause and cheers. The noise echoed throughout the halls of the Capital, and it took several minutes for the cheering to die down. Then speaking in a strong, calm voice, Wilson spoke of the insufferable attacks Germany had committed against the United States. He spoke of the need for the American nation to rise up, and take a stand against the tyrannical policies of Germany, and her Kaiser. He spoke of the need for America to mobilize its resources, and raise an army of 500,000 men if needed. Then, to give the war a higher meaning, he uttered what would become the war's most famous slogan: *"The world must be made safe for Democracy!"*

When Wilson concluded by asking congress for a declaration of war against Germany, he received the greatest ovation of his life. Later that night he said, "Think of what they were applauding. My message today was a message of death for our young men. How strange it seems to applaud that." Four days later at 3:00 AM on April 6th, 1917, congress obliged him and voted to declare war on Germany, 455 to 56. Once again, America was at war, and a generation of young men would soon be getting draft notices in the mail, telling them to report for military service. One of these young men was my grandfather.

How did this happen? Why was America at war again? How was it possible that just a mere five months before, America elected a president who was committed to peace, and now was asking for a declaration of war? To answer that, we need to look back at some history.

On May 29th, 1914 Grandpa turned eighteen years old. The following June the Archduke Francis Ferdinand of Austria-Hungary and his wife were gunned down by a Serbian nationalist in Sarajevo, Bosnia. This triggered what will become known as the Great War, or World War I, as Germany, Russia, Austria-Hungary, France, and Great Britain fulfilled their treaty

28

obligations, and rushed into what is probably the most insane war in history. The outbreak of the war surprised most Americans, and President Wilson made it clear the U.S. would not become involved, and remain neutral, "…in fact as well as in name."

In the years that followed, the application of new and deadlier weapons such as the machine gun, poison gas, and monstrous artillery created a slaughter on a scale the civilized world had never seen before. Folks in Oconee, and the rest of America would, over the next three years, read in their newspapers about the destruction of young men in the millions. Place names such as the Marne, Tannenberg, Verdun, and the Somme become synonymous with appalling horror and death.

The terrible weapons of the war made frontal assaults suicide, and both the allies (Britain, France, and Russia) and the Central Powers (Germany, Austria-Hungary, and Italy) began to dig in. Extensive trench systems were built by both sides, giving the war its most distinctive feature. As early as September of 1914, trenches began to be dug, and soon they stretched from the North Sea to Switzerland. With millions of men dug in, and the killing fields of Belgium and France crisscrossed by thousands of miles of trenches, the war settled into a frustrating stalemate. Faced with their inability to win a decisive victory, generals on both sides began to show an appalling lack of imagination, and stupidity. They began to believe attrition was the key to victory. The math was simple, whoever ran out of men first loses! So the war became a meat grinder, and the men, cannon fodder.

In their attempt to crush each other, both sides tried to starve each other out. Great Britain used her superior navy to blockade German ports, and prevented all countries, enemy and neutral alike, from trading with Germany. American ships were stopped, boarded, and searched. Goods suspected of being contraband, even foodstuffs, were confiscated. This was an obvious violation of international law, and freedom of the seas. Wilson was infuriated. However, a combination of allied propaganda, and increasing ties with Great Britain contributed heavily to a growing American sympathy with the allies. While the blockade kept us from trading with Germany, our economic losses were now compensated for by the increase in trade with the allies. The economy boomed, as our farms and factories produced food and weapons for the allies.

The war was good for business, and business was good. In fact our overseas trading surplus in 1913 was $690 million, and by 1916 it had risen to $3 billion. It was no accident that there were nearly eight thousand new millionaires in the U.S. the first three years of the war. In addition to our increased trade and profits, American banks began to float huge loans to the allies as their financial resources began to dwindle. By 1917, the allies owed the U.S $2 billion. Despite our stated neutrality, America had an increasing stake in an allied victory, and worried what would happen to their investment if the allies lost.

However, propaganda and economic ties were not the only factors to influence the United States. There was one additional, very important one that ultimately made Germany America's enemy. In trying to starve out Great Britain, Germany made a fateful decision. On February 4th, 1915, Germany announced that it would unleash a new weapon-unrestricted submarine warfare. Germany declared the waters surrounding the British Isles a "war zone", and any enemy merchant ship caught within the zone would be torpedoed and sunk on sight. In addition, Germany made it clear that the safety of neutral ships could not be guaranteed. Over the next few months, despite American protests, Germany sunk numerous ships in the "war zone".

Three months after Germany's announcement, on May 7th, 1915, the British passenger liner, the Lusitania, was sailing off the coast of Ireland headed for Liverpool, England. It carried 1,257 passengers, of which 159 were Americans. It also carried crates of ammunition. In the waters that day was a German submarine, or U-Boat, as they were called, prowling and looking for a target. It found one. At 2:09 P.M., without any warning, the commander gave the order to fire, and a torpedo packed with 290 pounds of explosives sliced through the water before slamming into the Lusitania with volcanic violence. Chaos reigned, and within eighteen minutes the great ship slipped beneath the waves of the cold Atlantic. The loss of life was appalling with 1,202 deaths that afternoon including ninety- four children, and thirty- one infants. Of the 159 American's on board, 124 perished. This was the turning point in American public opinion. While there was still a strong desire to stay out of the war, Americans' nonetheless began to perceive the German's as barbaric, savage, and the "Hun". A strong shift in American's perception began to take root as the country increasingly began to see the German's as the villain. Strong American protests followed, and Germany, fearing the loss of American neutrality, backed off its unrestricted submarine campaign, at least for a while.

In spite of recent events and the growing support for the allies, America's desire to remain at peace remained strong. Songs like "I didn't Raise My Boy to be a Soldier" reflected public opinion, and were extremely popular. In the 1916 presidential election Wilson won with the campaign slogan, "He kept us out of war!" With the end of the war nowhere in sight, and fearing what the future might hold, Wilson tried several times to hold peace talks. He met with no success. Then on the last day of January, 1917, events that would drag us into the war began to quickly unfold.

The previous year had been especially hard on German armies, and it now found itself on the defensive on the western front. Germany realized that if it didn't do something soon, its armies would be bled white, and they would lose the war. To them the solution was obvious. They would have to resurrect their policy of unrestricted submarine warfare, and starve Britain once and for all. German military planners calculated that if German U-Boats could sink 500,000 tons of shipping a month, Britain could be brought to her knees. The problem, of course, was that it risked bringing the U.S. into the war. However, it was a calculated risk Germany was prepared to take. Best case scenarios by their expert planners said it would take six to eight months for the U.S. to mobilize its resources, raise, equip, and train an army, transport it across the Atlantic, and put it into battle. Twelve months at the most. Time enough for the U-Boats to do their deadly work, and bring Britain to defeat. In effect, Germany was throwing the dice and gambling it all; betting it could win the war before America could do anything about it. It was a gamble that came incredibly close to paying off, for by the time the U.S. landed its first troops in France, Britain was down to six weeks of food. But the U.S. pulled off a miracle. It neutralized the U-Boat threat, raised, trained, and transported a two million man army, and drove the German government to an armistice. All of this was accomplished by November 11th, 1918, just over a year and a half after the resumption of unrestricted submarine warfare.

On January 31st, 1917, Germany announced its intentions saying it would sink any vessel bound into or out of any allied port, and it extended the war zone to cover the high seas. Germany wasted no time, and resumed its attacks the next day with the U.S. immediately breaking off diplomatic ties. Then Germany really blundered. In what became known as the "Zimmerman Telegram", Germany urged Mexico to declare war on the U.S. if we entered the war. If they did so, Germany would offer financial support, and assure the return of Texas, New Mexico, and the Arizona Territory. The message was intercepted by British intelligence on March 1st and the offending news was quickly publicized in the U.S. Wilson and the country were outraged. War fever began to grip the nation and the congress. Then on March 16th, 1917, U-Boats sunk three American ships without warning. That was enough for Wilson, and seventeen days later he asked for and got a declaration of war against the Imperial Government of Germany.

America was now at war. However, this was not to be just any ordinary war. As far as Wilson was concerned, if America had to go to war, it had to be for lofty purposes and idealism. This war would *make the world safe for democracy*", and it would be the *"War to end all wars."* Wilson, and the American people saw the war as an opportunity for the new world to fix the old, and create a better world where democracy could flourish, and autocracy extinguished. We were on a crusade, and America was going *"over there"* to save civilization. As the authors of *Shelby County Illinois in the World War* put it, "...were not our boys to establish a new order of civilization upon the face of the earth?"

This was the task my Grandpa and his generation were expected to accomplish, nothing less than the saving of western civilization itself.

Chapter III

Uncle Sam Raises An Army

"Uncle Sam", as he became known, was created by artist, James Montgomery Flagg. This well known recruitment poster was first used in WWI, but would symbolize patriotism in America's armed forces for generations to come.

The day after congress declared war, people across the country sat down at the breakfast table, opened their newspapers, and saw large banner headlines shouting that we were now at war. The news brought to a climax the tension that had been building up in recent months, and was met with an outpouring of intense patriotism that is hard to imagine today. There was almost a sense of celebration as American's shouted slogans like "On the Berlin!", and "Kill the Kaiser"!

Now that the country was at war, it had to be mobilized. Weapons and ships had to be manufactured, training camps set up, money raised, and public opinion molded. One of the first things the Wilson administration did was set up the Committee on Public Information. Its job was to create wartime propaganda, and fuel the war spirit needed to fight the war. Artists and writers were hired to create posters and slogans. Public speakers were employed to go out and give speeches to rally nationalistic emotions. They did their job well— a little too well actually. The war and its propaganda generated a hatred of anything German, which was often expressed in irrational and violent ways. For instance my grandmother, who was sixteen in 1917, once told me about a farmer southwest of Ramsey who had his barn burned down for uttering an unpopular remark. Sixty years later, she still expressed shock and disbelief that anyone could do such a thing. In another example of distorted patriotism, St. Paul's Evangelical Lutheran Church in Shelbyville "Officially, and without dissenting voice", banished the German language from all church services. The fact that there were elder members who did not understand English apparently made no difference.

As might be expected, the outbreak of war compelled thousands of patriotic young men to line up, and enlist in the service. However Uncle Sam wasn't getting the numbers he needed. Three years of reporting on trench warfare will do that I guess. In any case, President Wilson proposed a national conscription, or draft. Congress agreed, and on May 18th, 1917, eleven days before Grandpa's twenty-first birthday congress ratified the Selective Service Act. It would be the first draft in the country since the Civil War, fifty- two years before. Initially all able- bodied men between ages 21-31 had to register. Later the range was extended to 18-45.

Shelby County wasn't too different from the rest of the country when it came time to fight for their country. In *Shelby County in the*

World War 1917-1918 the authors wrote quite dramatically that "within forty-eight hours after the American dogs of war were unleashed Shelby county boys had offered themselves to their country and the world..." It also described Shelby's County's response as "...instant and unreluctant..." Well I can think of one young man whose response wasn't so instant or unreluctant. Grandpa apparently didn't get too caught up in all of the excitement. He told me that he hadn't even planned on registering for the draft- he was going to simply ignore it! However a Mr. C.P. Diefenthaler, who was one of the Oconee registrars, and who as Grandpa said, came from "very reliable people", encouraged both Grandpa, and older brother Henry to register. As Grandpa remembered it, Diefenthaler advised "I wouldn't pay you to go and register, but this is a serious matter." Indeed it was serious. President Wilson had announced on June first that anyone failing to register would be arrested, and subject to a year in prison. Duly impressed, Grandpa and elder brother Henry did what they were told, and along with ten million other men across the country, registered on the fifth of June, 1917. There were fears that the draft would provoke riots throughout the country, especially in cities with large German-American populations such as St. Louis. Given those worries and the seriousness of the situation, the country felt some trepidation as June 5th approached. But far from being a day of grim solemnity and riots (there weren't any), it was just the opposite. Secretary of War Newton Baker had encouraged communities throughout the land to make registration day "...a festive and patriotic occasion" Shelbyville happily complied.

To kick things off, Judge James C. McBride of the Shelby County Circuit Court suspended the session for half an hour while he and others attended the ceremony on the plaza before the county courthouse. A new flag from the state senator was raised, and a salute was fired. A bugler blew a martial call, the band played the Star Spangled Banner, and patriotic speeches were made. Afterwards Reverend Jasper L. Douthit gave the benediction, and then finally the registering began. Similar scenes were played out at several locations throughout the county.

The county was divided up into thirty precincts where the men could register. Oconee was one of the precincts that day, so Grandpa didn't have far to travel. Registration took place at an election polling station with the three registrars: Henry Hinton, C.P.D. Diefenthaler, and J.A. Hendricks presiding. The precinct opened early, around seven. Soon the men began to arrive, many on foot, often accompanied by family. Once there, the young men engaged in a number of the usual and tedious tasks, such as filling out registration cards and questionnaires. Each registrant had to provide his name, address, age, distinguishing features, and reasons, if any, for exemption. Once done, they were given a small green card as proof of their registration. The registrars would then sort them into one of five classes provided for in the regulations. There would be hearings, and decisions made regarding exemptions, as well as additional decisions made regarding the order in which they would be called for service. At a later date the men would be required to take a physical. It must've taken hours to process all ninety- two Oconee lads who showed up that warm summer day.

All told, 2,172 men from Shelby County registered for the draft that day. An additional thirteen were added later, making the official total 2, 185 men. As I researched this, some interesting statistics began to emerge. First of all, of the 2,185 men who registered, 1,174 of them had dependent relatives. In other words, 53 percent of them had families. The law allowed exemptions for those with dependents, and certainly many of them took full advantage of that. Most draftees in the U.S. were unmarried, with 75 percent of married men receiving deferments. Another interesting fact is that 192 men in Shelby County, or 8 percent, claimed occupational exemptions, while 760, or 35 percent, did not. Occupational exemptions would've been available for those whose work was considered necessary for maintaining military or national interests; Farmers, for example. Brother Henry was able to get such an exemption. Grandpa once told me how his family made the decision about who would put in for an exemption, and who would go if drafted. For whatever reason, Grandpa never explained, the decision was made that Henry would put in for the farming deferment, and Grandpa would go if called. How would a family make a decision like that? What a conversation that must have been. Amazingly, when relating this story to me, Grandpa betrayed no sense of anger or bitterness about the decision, and simply said it was "fine" by him.

On that momentous day, 9,660,000 men nationwide registered for the draft. A few weeks later, on July 20th, the first draft of the "Great Lottery" took place. Ten thousand five hundred numbered capsules were placed in a large glass bowl. Blindfolded so as to ensure impartiality, Secretary of War Baker drew out the first capsule. The number inside was 258. Throughout the nation in each registration district the men who held that number were the first to be called into service, and the building of the American Expeditionary Force began.

In the course of the war there would be four registrations total, nationally and in Shelby County. They occurred on June 5th, 1917, June 5th, August 24th, and September 12th, 1918, the last one taking place almost a month to the day before the war ended. When it was all said and done, 5,819 Shelby County boys signed up for the draft. 1,398 young men would actually serve in the military (these will be enlistees, as well as draftees). Over 1,300 were soldiers, fifty- six were sailors, and forty-two served as Marines. They served at Chateau-Thierry, Ypres, the Argonne Forest, St. Mihiel, and of course, the Hindenburg Line. They served bravely and well, and when the armistice finally came on November 11th, 1918, sixty of them would not come home.

Chapter IV

Drafted!

FIFTY-FOUR MEN FOR CAMP TAYLOR, KY., FEBRUARY 23, 1918

Grandpa second row from the top, (third from the left), and his pal Orville, 3rd row from the bottom, (fourth from the left) and their fellow draftees, the day they were inducted into the army – February 23, 1918.

Once the registration took place, there was nothing to do but go home, wait, and hope Uncle Sam didn't call you up and send you to war. Over the course of the next eighteen months, thirty- four groups of "contingents", as they were called, were drafted and inducted by the Shelbyville draft board. For Grandpa it would be a nine month wait between registration and induction. Time enough for tending and harvesting the spring crop, butchering the fall meat supply, and putting in a crop of winter wheat.

The first contingent was inducted on Sept. 5th, 1917. It consisted of only eight men, but thousands came to Shelbyville, the county seat, to see them off. According to *Shelby County Illinois in the Great War 1917-1918*, there was a "great patriotic demonstration" and the men were treated like heroes. In a routine that would repeat itself over the next fifteen months, they posed for their photograph on the courthouse steps, followed by dinner at the New Neal Hotel. Feted and fed, they later boarded a train for Camp Taylor, Kentucky.

In the months ahead, Camp Taylor would become the destination and home for five of the thirty- four contingents inducted in Shelby County-267 men in all. Not only Shelby County boys, but boys from Alabama, Indiana, Kentucky, Louisiana, North Carolina, Tennessee, and Wisconsin would make the camp's acquaintance. Named after President Zachary Taylor, it was located five miles southeast of Louisville, Kentucky, just across the Ohio River, and the Indiana border. Camp Taylor was one of thirty -two camps authorized by the war department to be built. Sixteen each in both the north and south. The camps in the north would be built around conscripts and volunteers, while the southern camps would house existing National Guard units.

The War department stipulated that each camp was to be built near a railroad on land consisting of anywhere from 8,000 to 12,000 acres, with a good supply of water. Of course there was a great urgency to get the camps up and running, and in what would become the greatest government project since the building of the Panama Canal, construction began immediately building the camp. Tremendous amounts of material, manpower, and organization was needed to get the job completed quickly. Each day of construction twelve trains, each pulling fifty cars of materials, steamed their way to the camps. Two hundred thousand construction workers were hired to build the camp, but even this was insufficient, and in many cases the soldiers themselves were put to work building as well.

Camp Taylor was established on July 18th, 1917 and it was

mammoth. It was built on 23,622 acres, consisted of 1,563 buildings, and had a troop capacity of 45,424 men. As stated earlier, men from many states came through the camp including 16,205 Illinois men. The camp would serve several purposes during its brief existence. It would train men for the infantry and artillery branches, and it also housed schools for officers and chaplains. It also served as a depot for troops. That is to say, troops would be trained there and then later assigned to wherever needed to other outfits. This would be Grandpa's experience, as he spent only one month at Camp Taylor before being transferred to Camp Sevier, South Carolina. When the war ended, it would serve as a demobilization camp to help process soldiers back to civilian life.

Before long, and often before the camps were finished, troop trains carrying their young, excited cargo headed for these camps. The sound of train whistles shrieking their arrival would be a common sound heard throughout the farms and cities of America during those days. Grandma would speak of her memory of seeing troop trains roaring through Ramsey with townsfolk by the tracks cheering, and waving to the soldiers. On days when the wind was from the north, she said she could clearly hear the trains from the farm, two miles south of town.

On September 18th, thirteen days after those first eight men boarded the train for Camp Taylor, the second contingent was inducted. This time sixty- four Shelby County lads assembled at the county seat. One of them was Grandpa's cousin, twenty three year old, John Henry Rakers. John's father, Henry Rakers, was Gerhardt's older brother. He lived and farmed on the northern edge of Oconee. I interviewed John in July of 1988, shortly after Grandpa died. He was ninety- five years old at the time, and living in Barry Retirement Home in Pana. Aunt Agnes first told me of John that summer, and I determined to meet with him, and learn of his experiences. When I arrived with my tape recorder, I introduced myself, and told him of my purpose for being there. Despite not knowing me from Adam, he seemed pleased to see me. He spoke slowly and with a soft voice, but his memory seemed sharp. I had been warned by Aunt Agnes that he probably wouldn't talk about the war, that the war had made him crazy (her words), but I found the opposite to be true.

John remembered getting his draft notice in the mail one day shortly after the June 5th registration. He was eager to go, although his father wanted to keep him out. Farm deferment maybe? In any case it was to no avail, as John had to go. John's eagerness to go was fueled in part by a historical debt he believed the United States owed France. He said "If it hadn't been for France, England would've whipped us..." in what he called the "American-England war" (American Revolution). We "paid them back" John said, "a hard debt we owed them!" Nothing was said about unrestricted submarine warfare, or the other issues that led to the war. To him it was simple; we owed France. He also said he believed in President Wilson's crusade to make the world safe for democracy, and to make the war, the war to end all wars. Like so many Americans of the day, he hoped it would happen, but was disappointed when WWII broke out twenty- one years later.

I found John's remarks surprising and fascinating. Here, seventy years after the war, John was expressing the popular sentiment of that time, an attitude that I had only read about in history books. History always runs the risk of becoming stale and dull when it's eventually reduced, as it must be, to the pages of a book. But to actually hear someone who was there and speak about it as John did, really does bring it to life. It made it seem recent, and relevant, like it just happened yesterday. Visiting with John proved to be one of the great experiences I had researching this book.

The popular feeling of the time was that we did indeed owe France for their aid in our time of need 140 years earlier. In fact when the first America divisions arrived in France in 1917, one American officer (not General John Pershing, as it often mistakenly claimed) proudly proclaimed, "Lafayette, we are here!" Lafayette, of course was the French aristocratic hero, who gave his assistance to the American cause during the revolution. That proud announcement signified the repayment of that debt. It was also the source of some soldier humor. There's a story about some bloodied and bruised veterans of the 16th U.S. Infantry, who, when passed by some new recruits, shouted out, "We've paid our debt to Lafayette, so who the hell do we owe now?"

Dutifully, John made his way to Shelbyville for the induction. The night before, the men were housed in the jockey quarters of a local racetrack, where John was quickly introduced to one of the vices of army life-gambling. Ever the county boy and right off the farm, he was stunned to see his fellow inductees throwing dice. It tickled me to hear him tell about it. For despite the passage of so much time, he still sounded amazed, and mischievous at what he saw, like a naughty little boy who got away with something.

The next day a parade with a band was held in their honor, and like previous, contingents, they had their photograph taken on the courthouse steps. Later, they had a meal at the Neal Hotel, and then were marched to the train station. The train took them to Louisville, Kentucky, arriving about midnight, and the new recruits, no doubt exhausted, promptly went to sleep on their new straw beds. The next day the trip continued, eventually reaching Camp Taylor. After a month of training, John was transferred to Camp Pike, Arkansas for more infantry training, then onto Charlotte, North Carolina. Here he was assigned to the 4th Division, 39th Infantry, Company L. He shipped out for France in May, and by that summer would be in combat.

On Saturday, February 23rd, 1918, nine months after their June registration, the fourth contingent of inductees gathered in Shelbyville. This completed Shelby County's first quota for 160 men. In it were fifty- four young men, including Grandpa, his good friend Orville Hinton, and brother, Miles. Although a year younger, Grandpa had been friends with Orville since childhood. Both grew up on a farm and attended the same two story, red brick, grammar school. The two of them possessed some musical ability as well. With Grandpa on the accordion and Orville on the fiddle, they often provided music for local barn dances. A little over an inch shorter than Grandpa, Orville had a slight build, angular face and friendly blue eyes. He also had a mind for numbers, which he put to good use as a book keeper at the Oconee Bank. As fate would have it, both would find themselves assigned to the same division when they went to war, further cementing their long friendship.

All three said their goodbyes on Friday, the day they left.

Grandpa spoke of going by the Oconee Bank, where the banker Mr. Warner told him goodbye. Other friends and neighbors came by also to say farewell, and wish him luck. Grandpa never told me, and I never thought to ask, how his family handled his departure. Certainly it would've been an emotional farewell. Many years later, Orville wrote an account of his experiences called *World War I Remembered*, and in it he recalled that the community got together to give him a going away party. As a token of their esteem, they gave him a gold watch. There was some hard feelings in the Hinton family that day. One of the registrars on the draft board was Harry Hinton, Orville's uncle. Presumably, so as not to show any favoritism, both sons from the Hinton family were drafted. As might be imagined, their parents resented it deeply. Perhaps as a concession to the aggrieved parents, Miles would not depart the same day as Grandpa and Orville. According to Orville, the departure of two sons was just too much for the Hinton parents, so the draft board agreed to split their departure. Miles would leave a day later.

Other than a few poignant anecdotes, Grandpa never did reveal much about what happened the day of his induction. However, one June day in 1988, I was in Shelbyville doing some genealogical research at the Library. My recollections aren't complete here, but apparently I was directed to the basement where, much to my delight, I found a treasure trove of information. Here I found materials that would add so much detail to Grandpa's experiences. I found books such as *The History of Shelby County in the World War 1917-1918*, and a history of Grandpa's regiment, the 119th Infantry. But without a doubt, the best discovery were the rolls of microfilm of the local newspapers published at the time of the war, *The Shelbyville Democrat*, and *The Shelbyville Daily Union*.

Quickly I fumbled through the rolls until I found one for February, 1918. With growing excitement and anticipation, I scrolled through the pages, looking for the Feb. 23rd edition. Finally I found it, and as I hungrily read the article, I felt transported back in time to that winter day, when Grandpa went to war. Thanks to those old newspapers, I can reasonably reconstruct the events and atmosphere of that day. What a day that must have been for Grandpa and those other men. Reading those articles, I got a sense of the patriotism, pride, sadness, and even humor that marked that, and the following days. Surely what Shelbyville experienced that day was a microcosm of the American experience in the Great War.

Grandpa, Orville, and the rest of the contingent arrived in Shelbyville on Friday, February 22nd. It was Washington's Birthday, a detail Grandpa accurately remembered when he spoke of that day. Speaking of which, as I did my research, I was more than once impressed by the fact of how Grandpa's facts often squared up with what I read. He had an amazing memory, and it was fun to see his memories validated by the various sources I used.

According to the *Daily Union,* all but three men showed up that morning, but arrived later on another train. In any case, at 3:00 PM they reported to the local exemption board for roll call. After the chairman of the board, Mr. William H. Chew, went over some necessary instructions, the men were divided up into six squads, each under the authority of a corporal. Grandpa and Miles (who apparently left Oconee that day after all) were assigned to squad #6, and Orville squad # 3. W.E. Rominger was designated by Mr. Chew to be captain of the contingent. The men were given tickets for meals and lodging, as well as a badge that said "Local Board, Shelby County, Ill." Then in a wonderful display of patriotic support, the ladies of nearby Clarksburg gave all the men new homemade sweaters.

The men's departure would not take place until the next day, so they were put up at the Neal Hotel. In a rather quaint phrase, reflecting the period I think, the *Daily Union* found it worth noting that the hotel lodgings were provided, "...*at the expense of the government.*" Now there is a phrase you don't hear anymore! I was tickled when I read this, as it could not have been much of an expense, compared to what was to come, and what we see today. But apparently in 1918, government spending like that was rare enough that it warranted special comment.

The men were considered guests of the Shelbyville Commercial

Club, who was responsible for organizing the entertainment and celebrations. At 7:30 that night the men were entertained by the local Boy Scouts at the Shelbyville High School auditorium. Unfortunately, the paper does not say what the Boy Scouts did that was so entertaining. Two hours later at 9:00 P.M., the contingent was treated to a basketball game between Sparks Business College, and Eastern Illinois Normal School of Charleston. In a later article, the paper described the game as "scrappy", and a "free for all". Apparently the game got pretty heated, and a fight broke out. A sheriff, policeman, and numerous spectators rushed onto the floor to restore order, but not before there were several black eyes and bloody noses. Sparks won, 42-28.

The next day, Saturday the 23rd, was the big day. This would be the day Grandpa, Orville, Miles, and all the rest would leave Shelby County as civilians, and not return until fourteen months later as veterans. The men were up early, and reported to the courthouse at 7:30 for final instructions from the exemption board. Shortly afterwards a local photographer, a Mr. Akenhead, had the men assemble on the north side of the courthouse for a group photograph. It was reported however, that one individual, apparently wanting nothing to do with it, refused to pose with the rest. Despite that, the photo was taken, and it was later published in the March 7th edition of the *Shelbyville Democrat.*

What a thrill it was to discover that photograph! I immediately sought out Grandpa, finding him towards the left, near the top row, looking straight at me. Orville stands two rows below him. All of the men are gathered on the steps with their bags collected in front of them. Most are wearing heavy winter coats, and they have their badges pinned on, just as they were instructed. A few chose to wear a tie, and every man is wearing a hat or cap. A few look very dapper, apparently wanting to put on their best for this important occasion. Others look more practical, farmers probably, and many of them are wearing sweaters. Could these be the ones the patriotic ladies of Clarksburg gave them? One man at the top of the photo is proudly holding Old Glory. Looking at their faces, it's difficult to draw any conclusions. A

46

few, such as Grandpa and Orville, are smiling, but most look passively into the camera. One can't help but wonder what they were thinking that cold February morning.

While the men were being debriefed and photographed, the Commercial Club, all one hundred strong, were assembling at the corner of Main and Broadway, getting organized for the parade. This was no small affair. The whole community had turned out, and businesses were to be closed for an hour and a half. The members of the club wore their badges, and one man was chosen to carry the flag. The Boy Scouts, along with hundreds of citizens, formed up with the marshal of the day. Meanwhile the band played several numbers, adding to the excitement of the morning. Finally at 8:15, all was in readiness, and the parade began.

Led by the band, the procession marched down Main Street to the public square where they were joined by the draftees and exemption board. The morning air was filled with the cheers of hundreds of onlookers, as they marched on foot or rode in cars, with the parade snaking its way west onto Broadway. After reaching the end of the street, the parade turned around, and retraced its route back up Broadway to Washington Street. Here the parade turned and marched south to the "Big Four" train station. To show their support, the crowd began to carry the men's baggage. Grandpa remembered a local undertaker named Kennedy carrying his to the depot. Once at the station, the band played some more "martial selections", and as the *Daily Union* put it "friends and relatives of departing soldiers gave them a hearty farewell that was as cheerful as the circumstances permitted." It was 9:15, and the train, right on schedule, chugged in from the west.

As Grandpa remembered it, the train was pulled by a "double header", that is to say two engines. It had been picking up soldiers all along the way, and its twenty coaches were loaded with men from Montgomery, Moultrie, Coles, Edgar, Clark, and Crawford Counties. I can just imagine the scene. The music, the cheers, the hissing steam of the engines as it pulled into the station. The newly arriving soldiers would've been staring with curiosity out the windows at yet another

47

town, probably looking for pretty girls. There would've been waving and hollered greetings, maybe even a few familiar faces would have been spotted. I doubt it would've lasted very long. The fifty- four brave lads would've been boarded quickly, and taken their seats. The whistle would've blown as the train slowly began to pull out of "Big Four". The boys probably leaned out of the windows for one last look, one last goodbye as friends, parents, and sweethearts ran along the train, trying desperately to squeeze out one more moment. Then suddenly, the train would've been gone, heading east, becoming smaller and smaller until finally, it disappeared in the distance.

As it headed east, there was a lot of joviality aboard the train. Pumped with emotion, there was talking, laughing, and singing. At one point a man spoke up loud enough for all to hear. "Always a spokesman in the crowd", Grandpa said. Obviously feeling reflective about the significance of the day the "spokesman" went on to say, *"Someday, somebody will come back to tell the story."* And as Grandpa remembered it, the men suddenly became very quiet and thoughtful. The only sound being the clickety clack of the train, as it carried them down the track to Camp Taylor, and their fates.

Chapter V

The American Expeditionary Force

(The A.E.F.)

By 1918 the U.S. has assembled a 4 million man army known as the
American Expeditionary Force.
(Photograph courtesy of National World War I Museum, Kansas City, Mo.)

The young men making their way to Camp Taylor were about to
become part of a four million man army. Up to that point it would be
the largest army ever assembled on American soil. It would exceed the
armies created by the Civil War, and would not be surpassed until the
Second World War. This new American army was organized around
three basic components: the regulars, the National Guard, and

conscripts. At the outbreak of the war, the regular army, that is to say a volunteer, professional standing army, had over 27,000 officers and men. The regulars would be supplemented by the National Guard- part time soldiers- which numbered 174,000 men. By 1916, roughly 77,000 of these guardsmen were already in Federal service helping General John Pershing track down and stop the cross- border raids of the Mexican revolutionary and bandit Poncho Villa. Once war was declared, the remaining National Guard units were activated for Federal service as well, bringing army strength to over 300,000 men. Still that was not enough. The draft, of course, would provide the rest of the needed manpower.

Draftees would be used to help supplement the regulars and National Guard units, but the vast bulk of them, or three-fourths of the army raised, would make up what was called the "National Army." In other words, this would be mostly a "citizen army." For every hundred men in the army, ten were National Guardsmen, thirteen were regulars, and seventy- seven belonged to the National Army. A knowledgeable soldier could tell the difference by the numbering system the army used. Regular army divisions numbered 1-20, National Guard units 26-42, and the National Army numbered 76-92. When it was all said and done, these three parts would become one of the largest armies in American history, with five out of every hundred Americans serving in it. Collectively it would be called the A.E.F. or American Expeditionary Force, and its soldiers affectionately called, "doughboys."

Nicknames for soldiers wasn't anything new in World War I. Throughout American history soldiers have been called numerous names. He was "Yankee Doodle" in the revolution, and "Billy Yank" and "Johnny Reb" during the Civil War. World War II of course, gave us "G.I. Joe." During the war soldiers of other armies had nicknames as well. The British were known as "Tommies", the French were the "Poilus" or the hairy ones, the Australians were called "Diggers", the Germans "Fritz" and so on. So how did the soldier of World War I become known by such a peculiar name?

Nobody really knows for sure, but there are several theories.

Some say it referred to the high pay the American soldier received. That his whopping $30 a month (which was also Grandpa's monthly earnings on the farm), made him feel loaded with dough! Others claim the term originated during the Punitive Expedition in Mexico in 1916. As American soldiers marched the desert roads on the border, they became covered in dust. Taking on the hue and color of the local adobe dwellings, Calvary men began to derisively call them "adobies," which in time became doughboys. Yet another story has it that the moniker emerged during the American occupation of the Philippines earlier in the century. As soldiers marched in the hot, sultry temperatures of the tropics, their uniforms became soaked with sweat. The hard marching covered them with dust, and combined with their perspiration, began to make the poor foot sloggers resemble bread dough-hence the name. So, as we say in the history business, "You pays your money, and you take your choice." There were some other names that competed for the honor such as "Sammies", in obvious reference to Uncle Sam, but when it was all said and done, by 1918 the name was here to stay. The American soldier of World War I would forever be known as "doughboys."

During the course of the war, an enormous amount of data was collected about the doughboys, and gradually a portrait of the typical soldier began to emerge. To visualize a typical doughboy, you need look no further than John George Rakers. The typical soldier of the war was white, in his twenties, had little education (Grandpa didn't go past the seventh grade), and was from the farm. In fact 53 percent of the army was made up of farm boys. He was also a draftee and a bachelor. The typical doughboy stood 5'9" tall (Grandpa was a half inch taller), and weighed in at 141.5 pounds. Sounds just like Grandpa!

The army as a whole, however, was largely a heterogeneous one, reflecting the increasing diversity of American life. Divisions were composed of Jews, Irish, Russians, Austrians, Hungarians, Serbs, Italians, and Poles. Forty- six nationalities were represented in this new American army, with over 18 percent born in foreign countries. There are stories told of German soldiers being utterly amazed and confused by the ethnic diversity of the American soldier. Even Native

Americans joined up with over 12,000 Indians of various tribes serving. An interesting fact from the war is that approximately twenty-six years before the famous Navaho code talkers of WWII were utilized, the A.E.F used Choctaw Indians for similar purposes. Despite the growing ethnic diversity of the U.S., and the A.E.F., I doubt Grandpa would've seen much of it. Those various immigrant groups would've been found mostly in eastern cities and not Shelby County, Ill. Nor would he have seen much diversity in the 30th Division, where he was later transferred. The 30th was mostly made up of boys from the Carolina's and Tennessee, and a quick perusal of their roster shows a collection of largely English, Irish, Scottish, and German names. I believe Grandpa, and the others would've been pretty much insulated from that experience.

There were African-Americans in the A.E.F. as well, but it was far different in 1918 than it is today. Blacks had been allowed to officially serve since the Civil War fifty -three years before, but only in segregated units. The A.E.F. would be no different, and their treatment of course was abysmal. Prejudice regarding black's innate abilities led to their exclusion from the Navy, Marines, and the young fledgling Army Air Corps. However, Blacks' were allowed to serve in the army, and thousands saw combat in France. One of the most notable Africa-American units was the 93rd Division. Interestingly they were loaned by General Pershing to the French, and fighting under French command they distinguished themselves in battle. But the truth of the matter was, most African-American Doughboys served in labor battalions (150,000 out of 200,000) building roads, bridges, moving supplies, and so forth. If Grandpa saw any black servicemen at all, it would've most likely been in the capacity of port stevedores, or laborers.

Another distinctive feature of this new American army was that it would be the first "tested" army in American history. Human psychology was a relatively new field in 1917. As such, it occurred to someone that the collection of so many men would provide an excellent opportunity to collect all kinds of psychological data, and possibly put it to practical use. For example it could be used to measure intelligence and help determine the appropriate military assignment, or promotion. Hence, beginning in May of 1918, the military began psychological testing of the men, and by January of 1919, more than a million and a half had been examined.

The American Psychological Association created two tests: Alpha for those who could read, and Beta for those who could not. Literacy, by the way, was another issue for this army. Many couldn't read, and the army took it upon itself to try and educate these men. Many resisted. There is a story of one doughboy who fought against it, arguing that he was going over there to shoot Germans, "not write them letters!" In any case, the tests were given and the results were, to say the least, interesting, often appalling, and sometimes simply hilarious. Being new at this, the association fell into the common trap of creating tests full of bias that reflected a person's socio-economic background more than their actual intelligence, with predicable results. It was found for example that 47.3 percent of whites, and 89 percent of African-Americas who took the test were mentally below the age of thirteen! As the Historian Edward M. Coffman put it "Either this pioneering testing venture was invalid, or most American men in their twenties were very stupid." Imagine a country boy or tough city kid being given a question like this....

Mauve is the name of a _____

A. Drink B. Color C. Fabrics D. Food

The answer, by the way is B, a color in case you didn't know. Or imagine them being asked to look at a picture completion task of a tennis court, and knowing that the net was missing. It's no wonder they got the scores they got, and it's hard to imagine how it could've been any use to them. But use them they did, and surprisingly the results were used to determine promotions. They found that corporals tended to score higher than privates, sergeants higher than corporals, and officers higher than sergeants. I can only speculate how Grandpa did on his tests, but considering he eventually made corporal, I figure he must've been dumber than some, and smarter than most. By the way, in another reflection of the times, the *Daily Union* proudly reported in its March 30th edition that Miles Hinton scored 314 points out of 400 on his psychological exam. Can you imagine newspapers publishing private information like that today?

This new army was terribly unprepared. President Wilson believed neutrality required unpreparedness, so little had been done to get the country ready. As stated earlier the regular army had only 127,000 men, putting us just behind Portugal in military might. You realize how small our army was when you read that the French army lost approximately that number in April of 1917 alone!

Not only were our forces pitifully small, but it was woefully under equipped. We lacked tanks, and had only a paltry fifty airplanes. Incredibly we only had enough ammunition to last one day of battle. Even after American industry converted to war production, and the A.E.F. was engaged in combat, we were heavily dependent on our allies for supplies. A few facts tell the story. The A.E.F. used 3,499 pieces of field artillery, of which only 130 were American made. Out of 8,116,000 rounds of artillery fired during the war, only 8,400 were made in the U.S. American boys flew French airplanes, and drove British trucks and tanks. The shortage of military equipment, of course, made training the troops difficult. Recruits often did not receive uniforms for months, and would drill in civilian clothes. Some even wore blue uniforms left over from the Civil War! Weapons shortages was another huge problem, as rifles, hand grenades, and machine guns were all in short supply.

Ever resourceful however, the army improvised, and had recruits practice with wooden rifles until they got the real deal. I once asked Grandpa about this. He seemed rather amused at my seemingly naivety, and replied that of course, they trained on real rifles. His reaction surprised me, and I wondered if he thought that in my innocence, I still believed soldiers fought with toy guns. Of course I knew better, but I didn't press the point. Orville, on the other hand, recorded that he did remember training with wooden guns. Two very different memories. Considering that both were at Camps Taylor and Sevier at the same time, I think it's safe to assume that both did indeed drill with wooden rifles at one point in their training. In all likelihood,

Grandpa didn't understand my question. In any case, Grandpa did remember that when the men finally received their rifles, they were covered with cosmoline (a grease to protect against rust), and with a chuckle, recalled how on one occasion an inept recruit accidently fired his weapon while cleaning it, leaving a hole in the barrack ceiling.

Probably the most critical shortage we faced though, was time. The allies had been almost bled white, and were putting tremendous pressure on the U.S. to mobilize as quickly as we could, and get into the fight. Allied leaders made it clear that it was men they needed us to provide-they would supply the weapons and so forth, but it was American manpower they wanted, and the quicker the better! Adding even greater urgency was the Russian Revolution of October, 1917. It had taken Imperial Russia out of the war, freeing thousands of German troops, who could now be sent to the Western Front to help crush the allies before the U.S. could fully mobilize. Indeed, in the spring of 1918 the Germans launched their final offensives of the war with that very purpose in mind. The war was rapidly approaching a decisive moment, and time was running out.

Could America put together an army, trained and equipped to do battle in time to turn the tide of events? This was the million dollar question, and many had their doubts. It was estimated that it would take a year before the U.S. could even put in the field an army of just 500,000 men. The British General Staff was less optimistic, believing that only half that number would be ready by the middle of 1918. However, incredibly, and much to the astonishment of the allies and Germans alike, this county assembled an army of over four million men in just nineteen months! It was an astounding feat, and a testament to America's resolve when it is committed to action. However, such an accomplishment in such a short span of time came with a price.

It takes time to make a good soldier. The transition from civilian to soldier doesn't occur over night. He has to learn discipline, military courtesies, close order drill, care of arms and equipment, combat skills, and so forth. However, time was in short supply in 1917, and even shorter by the spring of 1918, when the German offensives began. Not surprisingly, the amount and quality of training the men received

55

suffered. Under peacetime conditions it was thought that a minimum of one year was necessary to properly train a soldier. Obviously, with a war going on, a year of training was a luxury; besides, Chief of Staff General Peyton C. March believed that these new circumstances didn't require a year. He argued that these new recruits were more intelligent and motivated than a typical recruit. Unlike peacetime recruits, who in all likelihood enlisted because they were unemployed, misfits, or both, these new recruits were motivated by a "righteous cause." As such, March believed they would apply themselves to their training with a single mindedness of purpose, and could quickly be made into effective soldiers. In his opinion, three months was enough.

General John J Pershing, who was given overall command of the A.E.F., strongly disagreed with March. In his estimation more time was needed to properly train these soldiers. Eventually it was decided that a recruit was to get six months stateside training, two additional months in France, and finally, spend one month in a quiet sector of the line, before being committed to combat. It was a goal that, as time went by, was rarely met.

By the middle of 1918, a soldier was lucky if he got that much training. By that time there were roughly 325,000 doughboys in France. Other than some small engagements, they had not seen major combat yet. Then on March 21st, one day shy of a month after Grandpa's induction, the Germans launched the first of what would be five monster spring offensives. This was it. This was to be the knockout blow to win the war before American troops could make a difference.

It was now or never, and it had a huge impact on training.

Training was accelerated to try and meet the crisis. Doughboys began to receive three, even two months of training. Grandpa's case was all too typical. Consider the following: He was inducted on February 22nd. One month later on March 22nd, the day after the spring offensives began, he was transferred to the 30th Division at Camp Sevier, who was already in a state of accelerated training. There, he trained throughout April. By early May, he was aboard a transport headed to France, and by late July, he was at the front. So much for six months stateside training! If there was any consolation in this, it's that the division he joined already had nearly eight months of training. Plus they were a National Guard unit, so at least he was with people who had some experience.

General John Pershing

Still, compared to some guys Grandpa was lucky! Consider the 90th Division. When they stepped ashore in France in June, 1918, it was estimated that an astonishing 65 percent of the men had only four weeks, or less, of training! There are shocking stories of troops arriving in France who had never fired a rifle. In fact, by the summer of 1918, there were two divisions in France that had regiments in which roughly four out of ten men had never fired their weapon. There are even accounts of desperate doughboys who were so poorly trained they would pay veterans $5.00 to teach them how to properly load their own weapon. Grandpa never said if his abbreviated training made any difference, but it must've of. I can't help speculate what role this played in the extremely high casualties the A.E.F experienced.

So what kind of training did the doughboy receive? The last major war on the scale of WWI that American was in was the Civil War, and warfare had changed considerably since then. We had no real experience with modern warfare. When WWI began, the European powers had charged into battle, much the way we had in the 1860's. There was music, colorful uniforms, flapping flags, and attacks by massed formations, and on horseback. There was still an aura of romance, gallantry, and chivalry about war. But four years of butchery had changed all that. Poison gas, tanks, flame throwers, and machine guns had stripped warfare of its pretenses of being civilized and noble. It was now filthy, murderous, and meaningless. What had started out as a war of movement, quickly became static, with all the armies living like animals in the trenches. Perhaps it can be said that war is more tolerable when there is movement. The advancement of armies and the occupation of territory can create a sense of progress, accomplishment, and hope of eventual victory. It's good for morale. But a static war can have the opposite effect. When a war bogs down, especially if the armies have to dig in, it can have a debilitating effect on the poor solders who have to suffer through it. Trench warfare can become a daily grind of boredom, filth, mud, and death. In addition, attacking the trenches was an exercise in futility, since by its very nature the advantage is with the defenders. Frontal attacks become little more than suicide missions with battlefield success often measured in yards. Thusly, modern warfare was a hell on earth, and the doughboys had to be trained for it.

Surprisingly, General Pershing didn't believe that trench warfare should be the focus of the soldiers training. Nearly four years of trench warfare had convinced him that it was a "meat grinder" and "defeatist." Additionally, even though artillery and the machine gun dominated the battlefield, he was convinced that marksmanship and bayonet training would ultimately carry the day. While some training in trench warfare

58

would be necessary, given the realities of the battle field, the American soldier must be properly trained for the day, hopefully, when the trenches were broken through. Pershing was not about to assemble a four million man army, only to see it rot and die in the trenches. "Victory could not be won by the costly process of attrition" he wrote, "but must be won by driving the enemy out into the open, and engaging him in a war of movement." If that wasn't clear enough he also wrote "We're not going to win this war by slugging it out in the trenches. At some point, we must break the Hindenburg Line, and when we do, I want us to know what to do when we get in the open."

To accomplish this the doughboy's training would stress discipline, individual marksmanship, bayonet training, and small-unit mobile tactics. Men who could "shoot and salute" would be the order of the day. I have to wonder though, what made Pershing think he could do what the allies had failed to do the last three years? Was it faith in the American fighting man? Would sheer overwhelming numbers do the trick? Did he sense that the German army was just about spent? Was it all of these? Plus how could he reasonably expect what was largely a quickly, and often poorly trained army, to fulfill his plans? In retrospect it seems impossible. Whatever was the source of his faith, in the end, he was right. Because by the fall of 1918, after having assembled in France a two million man army, the A.E.F. would participate in the largest offensive of the war, and indeed break the famous Hindenburg Line. I'm proud to say my grandfather was part of that monumental and historic effort.

Chapter VI
Camp Taylor

Private Rakers at Camp Taylor, Ky., the winter of 1918

After leaving the cheering crowds of Shelbyville, the 386 young Illinois draftees would spend the next fourteen hours traveling through the Illinois, Indiana, and Kentucky countryside. Other than the "spokesman" story, Grandpa never said anything more to me about that trip. However, just like the induction ceremony we can relive that train ride, thanks to the Shelbyville newspapers and the correspondence of some of the men who were there.

Reading those articles, I kept getting the feeling that the trip was an opportunity for a good time. It's easy to imagine. All these young men, most of them just off the farm, were going off on the adventure of their young lives. I'm sure most of them had not been too far from home before, and certainly the thought of seeing new sights and having new experiences pumped them up. There must've been a giddy sense of freedom and adventure. In every town they passed, they were treated as heroes. They were on a crusade by God, and they were going to save America, *and* western civilization! It must have been heady stuff, helped along perhaps, by a drink or two? It was noted in the *Daily Union* that one man arrived at Camp Taylor drunk. It discreetly didn't reveal his name, but it did announce his hometown of Paris, Ill. You just know that got the old hometown talking. Anyway, Grandpa's story notwithstanding, I think these guys were in a mood to cut loose and have some fun.

One of the men on the train was J.C. Starkey, a Y.M.C.A secretary from Mantoon, Ill. He wrote an article about the trip for his local paper, and it was reprinted in the February 26th edition of the *Daily Union*. In it, he describes an atmosphere where the men "were far from downhearted" and were singing throughout the train. He admitted that the music wasn't "classical", but was nonetheless greatly enjoyed by the men. At one point during a delay, somewhere in Indiana, he described an impromptu concert the men put on. The men gathered on the station platform, and led by a man named Tony and a cornetist, they performed a concert of patriotic songs. Wouldn't you love to know what they were singing?

World War I produced a lot of songs. Some of them quite memorable to this day. There was "Mademoiselle from Armentieres", "Oh How I Hate to Get Up in the Morning"," You're in the Army Now", and of course the big hit: "Over There."

Over there, over there,
Send the word, send the word, over there.
That the Yanks are coming,

The Yanks are coming,
The drums rum-tumming
Everywhere!
So prepare, say a prayer,
Send the word, send the word to beware.
We'll be over, we're coming over,
And we won't come back til it's over
Over there!

It wouldn't surprise me at all if that's what they sang at that little concert. I could be wrong about this, but it seems to me WWI was the last war where American soldiers went off to war singing as fervently as they did. Certainly there were war inspired songs written during WWII, Korea, Vietnam, and even our current war on terror. Yet it's hard to imagine modern soldiers singing as lustily as they did then. I think it takes a certain amount of innocence to sing like that, and I think WWI was the last time we experienced that kind of innocence.

Apparently the men weren't content to just put on concerts. Further down the line at North Vernon, a squad of men formed up, and using "antiquated tin pans for instruments" put on a drill exhibition for the crowd. With their commanders barking out orders, the men marched back and forth, but as Starkey wryly noted, they were "hardly up to West Point" standards. The crowd, however, didn't seem to care and was greatly entertained.

Finally, at 11 o'clock Saturday night, the troop train rolled into Camp Taylor. The tired soldier boys got off the train, marched one and a half miles to be checked in, and were assigned to their barracks. W.E. Rominger, captain of the Shelby County contingent, wrote in a letter, that was later printed in the *Daily Union*, that the boys were "happy, but leg weary and sleepy." He added that while there were some complaints about the mud in camp, the men had "no kick to make." The men were issued three blankets, one comfort apiece, (no pillows) towels, soap, comb and brush. Afterwards, at midnight they had "their first army meal", and then went to bed. They were allowed to sleep till 6:45.

The next day was Sunday, and Grandpa said he fully expected to go to church, as he would have back home. But the army was his home now, and he got his first army lesson that day. They were in charge - not he! *"They took that clear out of our mind right there"*, he said emphatically, *"cause they had a job for us to do."* And work they did, for the rest of the day. Other than that the day passed uneventfully, but that night sickness immediately made itself felt. The *Daily Union* reported that seven men in one company came down with the mumps, and would be sent to a detention camp. Sickness was a real problem in those camps that winter, with thousands succumbing to measles, meningitis, influenza, and pneumonia.

On Monday the 25th, the men awoke to reveille, and had breakfast. Afterwards the men were given physicals, and by 10: am they were all done, and ready for vaccinations. "It was no time to go around slapping men on the shoulder" wrote Starkey. When the vaccinations were done, it was time to issue the men uniforms. Grandpa remembered that the men were marched to a hall, where a soldier, with no regard for sizes, threw coats and pants at the men. If the uniforms didn't fit, they were to trade with somebody, which Grandpa did. Finally he was able to find a uniform that "halfway fit."

The uniforms the men were issued consisted of the following: Olive drab wool tunic with a stand- up collar, wool breeches, wool shirt, wool overcoat, Khaki canvas leggings, hob-nail shoes, and what was called a campaign hat. The hats were wide- brimmed Stetsons with a high "Montana peak". They came with a colored chord wrapped around the crown, indicating branch of service: blue for infantry and red for artillery. By all accounts, the hats were very popular with the troops, being comfortable and practical, but regrettably the men had to give them up once they were overseas. Steel helmets were issued to the men in France, and when they wore them they had no place to store their beloved campaign hats. The army replaced the hats with a more serviceable wool "overseas cap", as it was called. It was collapsible, and could be easily folded and stored away in a pack to be worn later behind the lines. Despite being discarded, the army found another way the campaign hats could contribute to the war effort. They were cut up, and made into hospital slippers. When you look at old photographs of doughboys, you can essentially tell where and when it was taken, by what kind of hat he is wearing. If he is wearing a campaign hat, he's still in the States. (There are exceptions, however. The very first troops sent to France were still wearing the campaign hats), and if he's wearing the overseas cap, he's either in France, or just returned home. Interestingly, there are photos of Grandpa wearing both.

Eventually the men were issued their equipment as well. Grandpa would've been issued up to seventy pounds of gear, and was expected to haul it all on long marches, while wearing a wool uniform, no less! It must have been miserable. His equipment consisted of a backpack, in which he carried his mess gear, extra socks, underwear, toilet articles, blanket, personal items, half of a two- man pup tent, spare shirt, and rations. He also wore a web cartridge belt with pouches for ammunition, a canteen, and a shovel, or what the army euphemistically called an "entrenching tool". On top of all of this he also lugged a ten-pound rifle with bayonet, and when he got to France he would receive a gas mask and steel helmet as well.

Speaking of helmets, steel headgear was a fairly recent development by the time the doughboys showed up. All of the European armies had entered the war wearing soft, cloth headgear of some kind. The Germans did sport a kind of helmet called a "Pickelaube", a silly looking thing with a spike on top, but it offered no real protection really. Head wounds had become so numerous that by 1916 all the major armies were wearing their distinctive helmets. It's interesting really, because steel headgear was a throwback to the 17th century. In fact, some of the helmets had a strong medieval look to them. The helmet the doughboys wore was a shallow, bowl- like affair that was of British design. It was badly designed, as it offered no protection for the back and sides of the head. Nonetheless the U.S. bought 1.5 million of them from the British.

After being issued their uniforms, the men got down to the business of learning to be a soldier. Grandpa remembered the men being marched to a forty- acre field for training and exercise. As far as exercise was concerned, Grandpa commented that he "had no idea how." I gave no thought to this at the time, as it didn't seem important, but as I did my research I read how so many doughboys didn't have a clue about exercising. Grandpa's passing comment revealed that his experience was so typical of all those soldiers. World War I histories tell us that 25% of the soldiers were from the farm and rural areas. Many did not know how to play games. I suppose calisthenics would've been completely alien to them as well. Physical education classes were probably completely out of the realm of their experience, and frankly, I think farm work would've given them all of the exercise they wanted. Surprisingly, physical training and exercise for the doughboys included such games as leap-frogging, three- legged races, and tug-of-war, giving their training an aura more of a pre-school playground than an army camp.

Drill of course, would've also been an important part of their training. They would've learned how to march in step, and perform the manual of arms. This required a lot of discipline, and endless repetition. Very boring work I'm sure. We can get a realistic sense of what that experience was like, thanks to a wonderful letter written by former captain, now corporal, Rominger. It was published in the March 30th edition of the *Daily Union*. Here's what he had to say.

"And then there is drilling. Next time anybody growls about how soft we have it down here…advise him to borrow a shotgun, put on a pair of hob-nailed shoes, and heavy, coarse socks, woolen underwear, woolen shirt, and a heavy overcoat buttoned up to the neck. Let him get up at 5:45, make his one bed (which is pillow less), and hop out into the damp, foggy atmosphere, juggle the gun until hands and shoulders are sore all the time straining every nerve for fear he won't hear the next command. Then let him keep on his feet until 11:00 drilling and shouldering said gun and then take a little hike out to the Chautauqua grounds and march around the race track head up, eyes up and chest out with an occasional jog (double time) to make him keep his blood circulating-let him try this. Then he can come in and eat and smoke and wash his mess kit and perhaps receive his mail. He won't have time to read it though for its back to the drill around 1:15 and keep going until 4: pm then games."

INFANTRYMAN

Front and rear view—Full Field Equipment

Light Blue Hat Cord

Device

An American Doughboy

Private Rakers quickly learned he wasn't going to like drill, and eagerly looked for opportunities to get out. Consider the following stories. It was the second or third day of training, as he once recalled. The men had been lined up on the company street so the captain could address them. "If anyone here can run a typewriter" he barked, "step two paces forward." Grandpa immediately sensed an opportunity. The Rakers had an old typewriter on the farm, and figuring that "anything will be better than this" stepped forward the specified two paces. How simply owning a typewriter qualified him as a typist, Grandpa never explained, but clearly he was willing to try anything. The captain proceeded to take Grandpa upstairs to an office. Once there, he gave Grandpa a book, the likes of which he had never seen before, nor could he read. Grandpa failed to elaborate on this point. But all things considered, it was probably a typing book. Apparently wishing to test Grandpa's skills, the captain turned over eight to ten pages, told grandpa to type them, turned on his heel and left. Ten minutes later the captain returned, and discovered that Grandpa had typed only three lines! Furious, the captain hollered, "Is that all you've been doing?" "Yes sir!" Private Rakers replied. Realizing he'd been had, the captain ordered Grandpa back to the field and take his place with the other men. Properly chagrined, and in a hurry to get out of there, Grandpa "hit every other step going downstairs!" Thus ended Grandpa's clerical career—but not his search.

A few days later the men were lined up once again. Once again the captain was looking for volunteers. This time he wanted to know if any man could drive a team of horses, and if so, step forward two paces. *Drive a team of horses!!* Once again Grandpa sensed an opportunity, and this time he wouldn't have to bluff. Thinking that "this is right down my aisle", he stepped forward the specified two paces. And once again the captain (who you'd think would know better by now), went ahead and picked Private Rakers. Grandpa was taken to a horse barn and given a pair of khaki overalls, gauntlet gloves (it was cold he said), and a cap. For the next two days Grandpa was in his glory, doing nothing but driving a team of horses hauling cinders, chewing tobacco, and spitting. The "other guys had to do the work" he said smugly, "I just had to drive." His good fortune caused him to rethink his initial assessment of the army. Perhaps he had been too hasty in his rush to judgment. "I just had it made!" he crowed. "If this is the army I don't mind!" The memory of it caused him to laugh, but then I could hear the disappointment creep into his voice, even after all those years, as he recalled that it lasted only three days. "Then I had to go walking again", and walking is what he would do for the rest of the war, confirming I suspect, his original assessment of the army.

Given his aversion to drilling, it shouldn't come as any surprise that Grandpa was capable of a little deceit. Sometime later, after being transferred to camp Sevier, South Carolina, Grandpa decided enough was enough. He went to sick call one morning limping, and told the doctor he had a bad ankle. The doctor bought the story, wrapped the "bad" ankle, and confined Grandpa to the barracks for a few days. That, I think, pretty well sums up Grandpa's feelings about drill.

Grandpa's training consisted of more than just drilling of course. In keeping with Pershing's dictum to "shoot and salute" there was training in marksmanship and military courtesies. He also learned how to care for his arms and equipment, as well as his own personal hygiene. The men were expected to shower often. A large shed consisting of ten showers, with hot and cold running water was built for the men. However, some men apparently were averse to bathing on a regular basis, and the sergeants had to crack down. Rominger proudly noted that the Shelby County boys were not "backward in this respect." There would've also been training in mounting a guard detail, grenade throwing, first aid, gas mask and bayonet drill. All of this would make for a full day I'm sure, but there were also propaganda lectures on German atrocities to listen too. To make certain they understood why they were fighting, the troops got a steady diet of these tales. They would've been told lurid stories of the rape of Belgium, the murder of Catholic priests and the bayoneting of children. Blood curdling stuff to be sure, but as it turned out, mostly untrue.

If there was any compensation at all for all of the drilling, training, and lectures it was, believe it or not, the food! Rominger commented in one of his letters that drilling made a man hungry, and that the camp cooks were a "marvel". He even went so far as to say housewives back home could learn a few things from them. I'm sure the ladies back home appreciated that. The food was plentiful, with every man receiving 4,761 calories a day, a quantity European soldiers could only dream of. Second helpings were encouraged, but there were stringent regulations against wasting food. A man was expected to clean his plate. Their diet consisted of plenty of meat, mostly beef and pork. They were fed a lot of corn bread, brown beans, potatoes, cereals, dried fruits, and coffee. The men could supplement their diet with goodies purchased at the camp canteen, and many a soldier received candy, cakes, and cookies in their mail from loved ones back home. Rominger assured his readers that none of it would go to waste. No small matter as the home front was making sacrifices, rationing foodstuffs to meet the demands of the military.

Speaking of rationing. Grandma once spoke of her Aunt Katie, who was "so patriotic", and worked hard to comply with the food rationing regulations. For example, folks back home were to cut back on white flour, saving it for the boys. However Grandpa claimed he never saw a slice of white bread the whole time he was in the army. Makes me wonder what happened to it.

In the weeks that followed Grandpa, and the other Shelby County boys would've made many adjustments to army life. They would've pulled guard duty (twenty- four hours on, and four hours off), and done KP (Kitchen police), sweep, mop, and shine shoes. "Yes we'll all make good housewives when we come back home" wrote Rominger. They would've marched, camped, shoot, and learned to obey orders. Yet, of all the adjustments the guys had to make, loneliness was probably the worst. "Lordy, but a man suffers from that!" wrote Rominger. With surprising candor he admitted to waking up at three in the morning, and crying like a five year old. Even though these were grown men, thoughts of their mother often occupied their thoughts-especially at night. He encouraged folks back home to write "big, long, gossipy letters that tell us all the news that isn't published!"

Loneliness could cut both ways, and Grandpa's mother, Mary, missed him desperately during the war. Aunt Agnes related a story to me about how Mary would periodically disappear for a while. Gerhardt would send his daughters to look for her, and they would find her on the south porch crying. She worried incessantly. Grandpa would write a letter home telling them he was fine, but Mary would wonder if anything had happened since the letter was written. She worried so much she became sick. At least that's what the doctor said when he diagnosed her with stomach cancer. It quickly became her fervent wish and prayer that she would live long enough to see her beloved son just one more time before she died. Once that happened, she said, she would be ready to go. Then one day the family received a postcard with Grandpa's picture on it, that only contributed to Mary's anxiety. In the photo Grandpa is wearing his campaign hat and long winter overcoat. There's red, white and blue patriotic bunting in the background, belying Grandpa's demeanor. When Mary looked at the photo she was shocked by what she saw. And as Aunt Agnes described it, he looked "terrible", "pitiful", and "scared". Her son looked so unhappy that Mary simply broke down, and sobbed.

For Grandpa and the rest, Camp Taylor was an education. They learned about discipline, team work, comradeship, and loneliness. (Grandpa once told me the most important lesson he learned was to keep his head down) They learned how to take better care of themselves as well as a variety of domestic chores. They began to learn how much their homes, mothers, and families meant to them. But it was only the beginning. Grandpa and thirty –five other Shelby county boys would spend only a month at Camp Taylor. On March 22nd, exactly one month to the day from their induction, they would be transferred down south to Camp Sevier, South Carolina. Here at the foot of the Cumberland Mountains, the next phase of their military life would begin, and their education would continue.

Chapter VII

"Old Hickory"

Campgrounds of Camp Sevier, S.C.

Why was Grandpa, Orville and the other thirty- four Shelby County lads transferred to Camp Sevier, South Carolina? It's hard to say. Grandpa's personnel file, located at the St. Louis branch of the National Archives, might've provided an answer, but a devastating fire in 1973 destroyed those records. All that's left to do is speculate. To help me, I turned to *The Thirtieth Division in the World War*, a divisional history of the unit Grandpa and the others joined. It provided, I think, some clues as to why the transfer took place.

The winter of 1917-1918 had been a hard one in the camps. The location of Camp Sevier had been selected in large part because of the South's sunny, warm climate. However, that winter the country experienced an unusually harsh winter with heavy snows, sleet storms, and extremely cold temperatures. The unusually cold winter brought much discomfort to the camp as well as disease. Beginning in November of 1917, epidemics began to break out in camp, with troops being stricken with measles, pneumonia, and spinal meningitis. To make matters worse, in February small pox and mumps also broke out. Numerous soldiers were affected by the diseases, and entire companies (approximately 224 men) were quarantined. The hope of course, was to keep the spread of the disease to a minimum, but that proved very difficult. It was not uncommon for a new company to enter quarantine just as an old one was leaving it. Naturally the epidemics played havoc with the divisions training schedule, (mumps made gas mask training impossible for example) and was responsible for the deaths of many men that winter. It's quite possible that by March of 1918 the Thirtieth Division was in need of some replacements. Perhaps that is why those Illinois boys ended up in South Carolina. Actually Grandpa would've been transferred somewhere anyway. Camp Taylor's role was primarily to serve as a depot for the collection and training of draftees until it was time to assign them to an outfit. It just so happens they were picked to join the Thirtieth.

Many years later, Orville recorded for his family his reminiscences of the war. In them he recounted an interesting memory as to how this might've unfolded. As Orville told it, one day the men were drawn up in formation, and every other man was told to step forward. Those who did "were the ones that were sent overseas." Orville, and I assume Grandpa, were two of those who stepped forward. Brother Miles, on the other hand did not, and spent the rest of the war at Camp Taylor. I assume this happened at Camp Taylor, partly because of his reference to Miles, but also because the whole division, not every other man, shipped out of Camp Sevier the spring of 1918. Nonetheless, I think it's odd he would claim that this happened prior to going overseas, and not before their transfer to South Carolina. My guess is that Orville, who told this story in his later years, confused this with his transfer to Camp Sevier. On the other hand, perhaps he equated the transfer to going overseas, as he had to have known that the Thirtieth was destined for France. Whatever the case may be, it appears that bad weather, disease, and random chance all played their part in determining their fate.

Their journey south began at eight in the morning, on Friday, March 22nd. Grandpa never spoke of the trip to me, but thanks this time to the *Shelbyville Democrat* we can get a feel for what that trip was like. In its April 4th edition, it published a very descriptive letter written by fellow soldier Ray Kingston for folks back home. It's an interesting and revealing letter. That train ride was just one more experience that broadened those country boys' world, and his letter is full of observations I think a country boy would make. He noted the trees, the soil, the rivers, and the mountains. In particular he took stock of the farms, and inevitably compared what he saw to farms back home—with home of course, besting all.

On the morning of the 22nd, the men were lined up by two's, and marched one mile to the Southern Railroad. All thirty- six Shelby County boys occupied the second coach of the train. After the remaining seventeen coaches were filled with approximately 648 men, they pulled out at 10:00 A.M. Sharp. The troop-laden train traveled southeasterly throughout the day, reaching Lawrenceburg, Kentucky before taking a more southerly direction. Here dinner was served, consisting of beans, tomatoes, bread, and coffee.

Kingston described the country they passed through as mountainous, rough, and extremely rocky. Rocks seemed to be the defining feature of the Kentucky landscape, as Kingston mentioned it a lot. He noted the numerous great lime-stone quarries, the "light red sand color" of the rock covered soil, and miles of four foot rock fences snaking their way through the countryside. The train wound its way along cedar covered river banks where the waters "rippled" over beds of solid limestone. Hundred foot walls of limestone hugging the river banks caused Kingston to marvel at their grandeur. When they reached Danville they began to travel through tunnels blasted out of the sheer rock faces. Eventually by his count, they passed through twelve tunnels in all, before they left Kentucky. Finally they reached the Cumberland River, and as they left the Bluegrass state, the only compliment Kingston could muster was that Kentucky had "...some fine pike roads."

After crossing the Cumberland River and into Oakdale,

Tennessee, the men had their second meal, or "supper" as they would've said. After eating their tomatoes, bread, and coffee the men began to feel lighthearted. Kingston wrote that the men were having a "grand time" singing and "soaking in the beautiful scenery." It must have been beautiful indeed, with a mountainous landscape covered with silver maple and cedar pine trees. The soil, as ever observant Kingston wrote, was a deeper shade of red than what he saw in Kentucky. Breaking up the wondrous scenery however, were coal mines and oil wells. He couldn't get over the steepness of the Cumberland Mountains, as he cracked that he'd rather be in the army than try to farm the side of those mountains! He figured that if a man lost his balance he'd "roll a mile before he would stop!" The farms he saw were small affairs inhabited by simple huts, and farmed with mule drawn plows. His pride was evident as he boasted that the fields he saw would hardly qualify to be a garden back in Shelby County.

As they travelled southward, the elevation continued to rise. By that night, as the "dim light of the moon" shone overhead, they reached the Tennessee River, just north of Chattanooga. Once in Chattanooga, they were shifted onto another track of the Southern Railroad, and followed a more southeasterly course until they crossed the Georgia line. Here the land was less rough, swampy, and covered with the famous red Georgia clay. They rolled through numerous small towns such as Dalton, Rockmart, Dallas, and Austell, periodically taking on coal and water, or changing crews. After travelling all night the train finally arrived in Atlanta where a light breakfast of bread, meat, and coffee was served. Despite its simplicity, Kingston wrote that it was "relished very much." Here in Atlanta they were transferred to the eastern branch of the Southern railroad, and their journey took them even higher into the mountains. After passing through the town of Madison, they crossed the Savannah River, and chugged into South Carolina. The terrain continued to be extremely rugged, yet dotted with small cotton farms. It caused Kingston to reflect. "We never saw twelve acres of level land after we left Camp Taylor" he wrote. "Shelby County people live in a paradise if they only knew it." Around noon they passed through Liberty, South Carolina, and dinner was served: more bread, meat, and coffee. Then as the men ate their dinner, the final push was made, taking them through mile-high peaks, villages, and rock quarries. Finally, after thirty hours and twelve hundred miles of travel, the Shelby county boys arrived in Greenville, South Carolina, "tired and worn out."

It was raining when they arrived. Wet and weary, they marched thee miles northeast to Camp Sevier, crossed a sandy drill field, and waited in the wet as their tents were set up. After the men were assigned a tent (eight to a tent) and assigned companies, they had a chance to eat, ("They sure have good eats here") and go to bed. The next morning after breakfast they were issued stoves to put in their tents. Once done, they finally had a chance to size up their new home. What they saw was awfully impressive. Home was virtually a tent city of, according to Kingston, 40,000 men! There were a few amenities, such as fresh drinking water that flowed off a nearby mountain, and rumor had it that the good breezes kept the South Carolina summer heat from being too oppressive. As Kingston closed out his letter he noted that the men were treated fine except they were a "little blue" over their ten day quarantine. Disease, of course, was still an issue. Then in a patriotic flourish he winds up his travelogue by assuring folks back home that "...we are doing our share", and " we don't any of us expect to come home until it's over 'over there'." Statements which proved to be all too true.

Camp Sevier, or "*severe*" as Orville cracked in his reminiscences, was the home of what would become one of the most highly decorated outfits in the war, the Thirtieth Division. While it would, in the next seven months, earn a special place in the annals of World War I, it already had distinguished martial roots going back to America's beginnings. The Thirtieth came into being July 18th, 1917, when the war department ordered various National Guard units from North Carolina, South Carolina, and Tennessee to consolidate into one division. Some of those proud southern units could trace their history back to the Revolutionary War, the War of 1812, the Civil War (North and South), and the Spanish –American war. Many of the units had more recent experience, having just completed service on the Mexican border chasing the Mexican bandit, Pancho Villa. By the time the division was supplemented by young men from Illinois, Iowa,

75

Minnesota, North and South Dakota, and Indiana, it reached a strength of over 25,000 men*.

The division was under the command of a Major General. There were several who commanded the division throughout its history, but it would be Major General Edward M. Lewis, a West Point graduate, described as a model commander, who would lead it in battle. The division was divided into the 59th and 60th brigades of roughly 6000 men each, each commanded by a Brigadier General. Brigades were further divided into two regiments each, of roughly 3000 men each, as well as a Machine Gun Battalion. The 59th brigade as divided into the 117th, and 118th infantry regiments, and the 60th was divided into the 119th and 120th regiments, each commanded by a Colonel. Regiments were divided up into three battalions each, with roughly 1000 men each. For example the 119th regiment consisted of the first, second, and third Battalions, each commanded by a Major. Battalions were organized around five companies of about 200 men each. Each company was designated by a letter such as 1st Battalion; companies A-D, 2nd Battalion; Companies E-H and so forth. Companies were led by Captains. Companies were further divided into platoons and squads.

The division was also made up of a number of artillery units, field signal battalions, engineer regiments, supply companies, chaplains, medical and ordinance departments, and veterinary field units. Speaking of veterinary field units, there would have been over 6,000 horses and mules in the division as well!

Each man was assigned to a series of parts that contributed to the making up of the whole. Each part could be detached or assembled as needed, to perform whatever task assigned to it. Every soldier was expected to know the various parts he fit into, and how he fit into the big picture. Thusly, Grandpa would be assigned to the 60th brigade, 119th Infantry Regiment, Third Battalion, Company K.

*On paper, division strength was supposed to be 27,082 men, but in reality were closer to 25,500 men.

As far as I can tell, twenty-two of his thirty -six Shelby County comrades from Camp Taylor were also assigned to the 119th. The rest apparently were scattered throughout the rest of the division. Orville was one of those assigned to the 119th, but again there is some confusion. His discharge papers records that he belonged to headquarters (HQ) company of the 119th. However in his reminiscences he tells of belonging to a "light armored squadron". He was part of a mule- drawn, five man crew that operated a "one pounder" gun. These were so called because of the weight of the shell, and they were designed to knock out German tanks. Why his discharge papers didn't indicate that, I have no idea. In any case, the two pals from Oconee would end up serving together in the same regiment. Not that it guaranteed they would see each other much, after all there were 3000 men in the regiment. Nonetheless, they both enjoyed telling stories about the few times they did see each other-*overseas* as it turned out, and once even during combat. They never could get over the irony of that.

The same order that created the division also mandated that their training would take place at Camp Sevier. Located in Greenville County, it was situated on a plateau at the foot of the Blue Ridge Mountains, three miles from Paris Mountain, and six miles from the town of Greenville. Fittingly, it was named after the Revolutionary War patriot, and North Carolina's first governor, John Sevier. Covering 1,190 acres, the camp was large, but smaller than Camp Taylor. Initially contractors were hired to clear the land and build the camp, but eventually the soldiers themselves provided the labor, as more space was needed for the swelling population of troops. Unlike northern camps, which had wooden barracks, the southern camps used tents instead. Given the South's reputation for a sunny, warm climate, it was assumed the men would be plenty comfortable living in the tents. I imagine another factor the planners considered was cost, as tents would be cheaper, and quicker to erect than wooden barracks. The assumption backfired however, and as noted earlier, the south would experience one of its harshest winters, causing deaths, quarantines, and disruption of training schedules.

The tents were large pyramid- shaped affairs laid out along company streets in long neat rows. Originally eleven men were assigned to each tent, but in an attempt to slow the spread of disease, that number was reduced to eight. As a further measure against disease, Grandpa and the others were ordered to sleep head to foot. Primitive as they were, the tents did have two luxuries: wood flooring, and tiny inverted wood burning stoves. Following the relative comfort of Camp Taylor, Grandpa must've wondered what the hell he'd gotten himself into.

Of course there were a multitude of other buildings in the camp to meet the numerous needs of a growing division. The camp was built along the railroad lines with ten long warehouses and numerous magazines (ammunition storehouses) set along the siding. There were mess halls, bakeries, and bath- houses where a dozen men or more could shower at one time. For the sick there were infirmaries and a base hospital.

Camp Sevier Remount Station. Horses played a vital part in the early 20th Century Army.

For the malcontent there were guard houses, and a division stockade surrounded by an electrical fence. Horses and mules of course, were still an important part of this early 20th century army, so there were remount stations with stables and corrals. Finally there were post exchanges where a doughboy could spend his pay on cigars, cigarettes, candy, cold drinks, razor blades, hat chords, leggings and so forth.

There were also facilities set up for the men's morale. If Grandpa wanted to write a letter home, read, play billiards, or watch a movie, he had his choice of the Y.M.C.A., Red Cross, Knights of Columbus, and the American Library Association to go to. Or he could've visited the Hostess House and gotten a home cooked meal, or perhaps take a class. Doughboys with theatrical talent could participate in the divisional theatrical troupe, and perform in the camp's "Liberty" Theatre. Grandpa could've seen a wide range of acts, ranging from grand opera to burlesque. There were comedians, singers, and as a sign of the times, minstrel shows to be entertained by. Music, of course, was an important part of camp life, and would've been heard somewhere in camp on a daily basis. There were regimental bands who would put on concerts and perform music for special occasions, such as dress parades and the like. The Y.M.C.A. provided song leaders who would lead their khaki clad audiences in robust sing-a longs. Songs like "There's a Long, Long Trail a Winding", "Pack Up Your Troubles", "Tipperary", "Goodbye Broadway, Hello France", and of course "Over There".

Diversions could also be found in nearby Greenville. The focal point was the Imperial Hotel, a favorite gathering place for soldiers. On Saturday nights the hotel would host dances with "….the ball room being gay with the laughter of beautiful women, and colorful with the uniforms of the men from Camp Sevier." To help fun seeking doughboys get to town, the Piedmont and Northern Electric Railroad connected the town to camp. Traffic became so heavy that the railroad ran trains hourly during the weekdays, and every fifteen minutes on weekends.

In time as the days turned into weeks and the weeks into months, the men of the Thirtieth began to band together, and develop their own identity, a sense of unit pride, or what the military calls "Esprit de Corps". This wasn't unusual, and it's what every commander hopes for. To create a sense of pride and to distinguish themselves from everybody else, the divisions around the county began to invent nicknames for themselves. Eventually they would take it a step further, and for the first time in American military history, design shoulder patches with insignias that symbolized their divisional identity. It's a practice still in use today. A few are worth mentioning, such as the 1st Infantry Division, or the "Big Red One". Proud of being the first American division in France, first in battle, first to take casualties, and the first to attack the enemy, it wore a patch with a simple big red "one". There was the 38th Division who was known as the "Cyclone Division", because a cyclone tore through their Mississippi training camp. One of my favorites was the 29th Division, or the "Blue and Gray". The men came from northern and southern states, which of course fought each other in the Civil War. Their insignia was the Korean symbol "Yin and Yang" for good luck, and the colors were-you guessed it- blue and gray. Perhaps the most well-known was the 42nd Division, or "Rainbow Division", so called because the division was composed of men from twenty -six states.

The Thirtieth required a nickname too. One befitting an organization with a proud fighting history, and one that would make a statement about its toughness, and historical identity. The divisional history isn't very clear about this, but it seems there was a lot of discussion throughout the division about a fitting name, with ideas possibly being submitted. I can see it now. The men sitting on their cots late at night, or eating in the mess hall tossing ideas back and forth. I'll bet they took it seriously, like little leaguers choosing a name for their baseball team. After all, they were young, proud and aware, I think, of the role they were soon to play. I think they would want a name that would stand out and be remembered. What part Grandpa played in all of this, or if he even cared, I don't know, but several days after his arrival on March 26th, the division announced its decision. I'll let General Order # Seven speak for itself.

The army shoulder patch of the 30th 'Old Hickory' Division.'

"'Old Hickory' was the affectionate nickname of Andrew Jackson, famous American general of the War of 1812... (And resident of the Carolina's and Tennessee). The name 'Old Hickory' is selected ....as best exemplifying the sturdy fighting qualities of soldiers from North Carolina, South Carolina, and Tennessee who comprise the vast majority of the personnel of the Division. It is his (Jackson's) indomitable fighting qualities... the Division will emulate. The military history of the ancestors of the soldiers of this Division gives every reason for the world to expect great things of their sons. The 30th Division will, accordingly, be known hereafter as the *Old Hickory Division"*.

And so it was.

Late in the war, the 81st Division (Wildcat Division) created a shoulder patch picturing a blue wildcat insignia. It quickly started a trend, and eventually General Pershing authorized all of the major commands to design an insignia for their own troops. This occurred so late in the war, however, that for most units their patches wouldn't be made, or worn until the war ended. In fact most units didn't have one until they got home. The Thirtieth, of course, had its own insignia. The

Divisional history does not say when the patch was adopted, so I cannot say if Grandpa wore it overseas. There are no photos of Grandpa wearing the patch, but there is one of Orville. In fact Orville, or somebody, even painted the division insignia on his helmet. The question of course is, when did they get the patches? In any case, the insignia selected for the Division consisted of a "blue elliptically shaped letter 'O' on its side, surrounding a blue letter 'H' with blue Roman numeral XXX inside the cross bar of the 'H', with the 'H' superimposed on a maroon field."

When Grandpa and the others arrived on the 23rd, the German spring offensives were two days old. Consequently, training throughout April was accelerated and intensified. The United States was under enormous pressure to get the troops trained and overseas before the offensives broke the allies back. The men's mood at this time was described by the Division history, as "eager" and "anxious". Aware of the desperate straits the allies were in, the men feared it would all be over before they could get into the fray, and their training would be for naught. The men were straining to go!

While they waited for the news that would determine their fate, the men continued their training in open warfare, marksmanship, and bayonet drill. On April 8th, the division received one day of gas training. They were taught how to use respirators and participated in a mock battle that exposed them to a surprise gas attack. On April 18th the men were organized to be taught platoon tactics by veteran French officers, and on the 19th the various regiments were given advanced battalion problems to solve. However none of the latter was completed, because on the 28th all training came to a screeching halt. The moment they had been waiting for, training for, had finally arrived. "Old Hickory" was given their orders to mobilize –they were finally going "over there!"

Thus ended the second phase of Grandpa's wartime experiences. It was an extraordinary two months, filled with more experiences than folks back home would know in a lifetime. The world must've seemed bigger, more varied, even scarier than before. What must've Grandpa been thinking and feeling at this critical moment? Was he one of the "eager" ones "anxious" to get in the fight before it was over? Did he feel the "fever heat" the divisional history spoke of? Somehow I doubt it. Grandpa never struck me as the gun-ho type, and if his stories are any indication, he was a reluctant warrior at best. But a warrior just the same, whose wartime experiences were just warming up.

Chapter VIII

Over There!

Twenty-five ships traveled in convoys to transport the 30th Division to Europe.

In a great piece of understatement the divisional history recorded the following; "It must be remembered that the transportation across an ocean ...of an entire division together with their equipment is no simple matter." Indeed! Of all the overwhelming logistical problems the U.S. faced during the war perhaps the biggest was safely transporting two million men to France. It was a challenge made all the more difficult by two annoying facts; our shortage of transports, and German U-Boats.

The ship shortage was dealt with in several ways. German vessels unfortunate enough to be stuck in American ports when war was declared were confiscated. Other ships were leased from the British and French with American shipping providing the rest. Nonetheless, there still were not enough. The U.S. was so desperate for more ships it was willing to do some old fashioned horse trading to get them. Despite General Perishing's well known opposition to parceling out American troops to fight under British or French command, he found himself willing to make an exception. Fearing that the anticipated German spring offensive would create a crisis situation, he began to consider a British offer. In exchange for several American divisions, the British would provide the transports needed to get them to the front. After much negotiation an agreement was finally reached on January 30th, 1918. The British would provide the transport to get six American divisions to France and in return, get the use of those doughboys. And just so there wasn't any misunderstanding, Pershing stressed that the divisions were on loan to the Brits, and that he could recall them anytime he saw fit. Thusly the 30th Division was picked to be one of the divisions on loan to the British, and became in the words of historian Mitchell A. Yockelson, "borrowed soldiers."

Researching this gave me one of those "Ahha!"moments about Grandpa's experiences. His stories were often sprinkled with references to the British. For example, once when I was a youngster I told him about playing soccer at school. This caused him to relate how he saw British soldiers playing soccer during the war. He also told stories about being in British field hospitals, drinking with British soldiers, and firing a British rifle, and it made me wonder. Now it all made sense. Grandpa was one of those "borrowed soldiers".

The other issue of course were the dreaded German U-Boats. Prior to America's entry German submarines had taken a frightful toll on allied shipping. By 1917 it reached a peak of a million tons a month. It had gotten to the point where Great Britain faced the very real possibility of being cut off, and its population starved if something wasn't done about this underwater menace. The British eventually adopted the American idea of the convoy system to counter this threat and it worked. The idea was simple enough. Instead of sending vessels out singly without naval protection, merchant ships and troop transports would now sail in groups of anywhere from ten to fifty ships at a time. They would be escorted by a flotilla of ships such as cruisers, destroyers and sub-chasers, who would aggressively seek out the subs. The hunters had now become the hunted. As further measures to protect the fleets, ships were often painted camouflage to make themselves less of a target. Once the convoys entered the danger zones around the British Isles, they would begin to sail in a zig- zag pattern, making it very difficult for a sub captain to aim his torpedoes. These innovations were extremely successful and had immediate results. The first convoy sailed on May 10th, 1917 with the loss of only one ship. In June, sixty ships made it across without any losses at all. In short order the tonnage of shipping losses decreased dramatically, and what had been a very dangerous and anxious voyage was now a rather dull and monotonous affair. Fortunately for Grandpa and the division, the convoy system was well in place by the time of their voyage, and with one exception, their trans-Atlantic crossing, while memorable, was largely uneventful.

Shortly after getting their orders, the division over the span of several days boarded trains and headed northward towards Camp Mills, New York, and Camp Merritt, New Jersey. Grandpa's regiment, the 119th, left Camp Sevier in two detachments on May 6th and 7th. Cheering crowds greeted the division as they passed through North Carolina and Virginia. During stops in Washington D.C. and Philadelphia, Red Cross workers served the men apples, cigarettes, coffee, and sandwiches. The regiment arrived at Camp Merritt on May 8th and 9th and would spend the next three days there, getting organized and equipped for overseas service.

Their days at Camp Merritt consisted of inspections, instruction in aboard ship behavior, and indoctrination. There were movies about lifeboat drills and lectures about U-Boats. Each man was issued two aluminum ID discs (better known as dog tags) that contained their names, unit designation, and serial number. In the event of their death, one disc would remain around the neck of the deceased while the other was sent to Graves Registration Services HQ for filing. Soldiers were required to sign an address card to next of kin indicating that the vessel they had sailed on had arrived safely. The cards were kept at the port of embarkation, and mailed once a ship arrived at its destination safely. Soldiers also received their final pay in French francs and British pounds, to avoid unnecessary money changing later. Lastly, before a soldier was allowed aboard ship, he was given a final physical. Anyone with a contagious disease was not allowed to sail.

Time was also spent dividing the division into three different detachments for the next leg of the trip. One would remain in Camp Merritt, another would go to Philadelphia, and the third-which Grandpa belonged to- would travel to Boston. From these respective locations the regiment would ship out. The rest of the division would ship out of either New York City, Philadelphia, or Montreal. Finally, after all of the final hectic preparations and movements, the first of twenty-five transports set sail on May 7th.

Of the three detachments of the 119th, the Philadelphia detachment left first. It left Camp Merritt on the 10th and arrived in Philadelphia the next day. No time was wasted as they were marched immediately to the docks, and boarded the British steamship *Haverford*, departing at 2:00 P.M. Roughly two and a half hours later at 4:30 P.M. the *Ascania* carried the Camp Merritt detachment out of New York harbor. The third, which was Grandpa's group, left camp on the 10th and arrived by train in Boston by 10: A.M. on the 11th. They were marched directly to the docks, boarded the *Laomeden* and set sail by late afternoon.

The three transports sailed directly for Halifax, Nova Scotia, arriving on Wednesday, May 15th. All twenty-five transports would eventually concentrate there and form into convoys. The first such convoy, twelve transports in all, including the *Ascania, Haverford*, and *Laomoden*, set sail on May 16th. The second convoy would depart two weeks later on June 1st. The *Ascania* would serve as the flagship of the convoy with Lt. Commander Underwood of the British Navy serving as commodore. The convoy was escorted by the British cruiser *Cornwall* and a fleet of destroyers. Long, sleek, fast vessels, the destroyers offered the main protection for the convoy, and were the greatest fear for U-Boat commanders. Throughout the voyage they would circle and dart in and out of the convoy, hunting submarines, "like pointer dogs in a wheat field." Troops also played their part in protecting the convoy, as all took their turns doing U-Boat observation duty, something I remember Grandpa once commenting on.

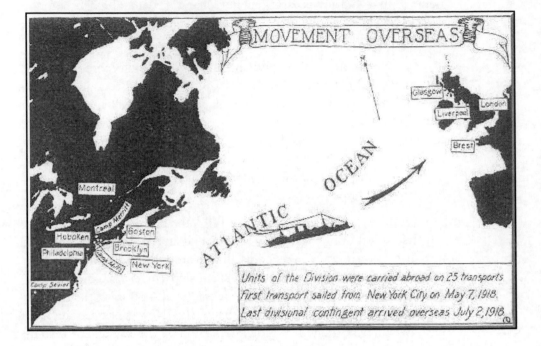

Ports of Departure for the 30th Division

For the next sixteen days that convoy would be home for those men, albeit a rather foreign home. The ships that carried the Thirtieth were of mostly British registry. One result was the men were served British food. American boys who were used to eating fried chicken, beef, pork, mashed potatoes, and warm bread were served tea, mutton, goat meat, hard tack, and orange marmalade. The orange marmalade caused particular revulsion as the men absolutely hated it! Much of it ended up at the bottom of the Atlantic. The division history noted the men's reaction when it recorded that the food "...caused first bewilderment, then hunger, and finally loud protests." Apparently this experience was universal among the doughboys. Complaints about the food being overcooked and unpalatable was common. There's even a story about doughboys briefly rioting on one ship, when they found out their Thanksgiving dinner would be the usual English fare. Some soldiers even joked about the food, saying they ate six meals a day; three down and three up.

Other than descriptions of the food, the divisional history is largely silent about the other ship board conditions. However, a reading of other sources makes it very clear that travel on these transports was an ordeal unto itself. Unfortunately, Grandpa said very little about it as well, but the unpleasant descriptions of the voyage were so widespread that I'm confident Grandpa's experience was very similar.

Accounts of the voyage consistently describe how crowded, poorly ventilated, and foul smelling the ships were, information noticeably absent from the divisional history. In their haste to get an army overseas, these transports were packed to the gills. The men slept in bunks that were often stacked three to four tiers high. The ships became so crowded in fact, that by the spring and summer of 1918 (the period Grandpa sailed) the men had to sleep in shifts. Between the crowded conditions, lousy food, and rough waters, sea sickness became a huge problem, and a salient memory for many a doughboy. Orville and Grandpa both commented on that. Orville claimed that the men were sea sick most of the time. Grandpa on the other hand, once said he came up with an unusual remedy to prevent it-ketchup! He would drink it to prevent getting ill, and it seemed to work for him. Encouraged by his success, he tried to convince others to try it, but they were too sick to even consider it.

The first few days at sea the ocean was rough with high winds, but by the 22nd the weather had calmed down. The voyage proved to be uneventful (until they reached the Irish Sea), with one unit even recording that"…the passage overseas was almost monotonous" Early on the men and crews settled into predicable routines, such as inspections and numerous abandon-ship drills that helped relieve the monotony, but even these began to lose their novelty. One gets a feel for traveling in these hulks when the division history almost poetically wrote:

"The voyage made a deep impression on the minds of the men.

The nights were particularly solemn and depressing. The big ships, dark as a tomb from end to end, plunged through the darkness, with not a sound except the throbbing of the engines."

On May 24th the convoy arrived off the coast of England and into the danger zone. While U-Boats had been an obvious concern, up to this point none had been spotted. The danger zone would be different. Realizing the risk they faced, abandon- ship drills were kept up, and more protection was provided. On the 25th Grandpa would've seen dirigibles, airplanes, and numerous sub-destroyers appearing, providing extra security through those dangerous waters. One can imagine the relief the men felt when you read in the 119th regimental history that the planes and boats "remained our best friends until the convoy landed."

Ironically, despite all of the extra protection, the most threatening episodes of the trip took place in these waters over the next two days. At 11:30 AM on May 26th, a U-Boat was sighted, but it quickly submerged. Destroyers moved in quickly and dropped several depth bombs and the sub wasn't seen again. On the following day, the 27th, the Haverford reported a sub attack on their ship. This attack was also driven off, and later that day, the Haverford and the rest of the convoy sailed into Liverpool safe and sound. Thus ended the sub threat to the convoy.

The rest of the division arrived in Europe at different times, at ports such as Glasgow, Scotland. Only one ship, the *George Washington*, sailed directly to a French port. The last of the division would not arrive until July 2nd. Certainly the men of the first convoy were eager to get off those ships, but they wouldn't do so until 5: PM. Their stay in England would be very brief, just long enough to get them to the front. Just the same, the British wanted to let them know they were welcome and every man was given a facsimile letter of welcome, signed by King George V. After debarking the men marched a short distance to their trains, which left at 10:00 P.M. for Dover, the main channel port for the movement of troops to France.

The trains passed through London around midnight, and arrived at Dover around eight the next morning. At eleven o'clock, the 119th regiment began to move by small detachments in channel steamers across the English Channel to Calais, France. It was during this crossing that another incident occurred that Grandpa would tell me about, and which also happened to be written about in the divisional history. As the steamer carrying Grandpa approached the Calais harbor, it rammed into an outgoing vessel. Grandpa said he saw it coming, and quickly put on a life jacket and grabbed a pole to hold onto. As Grandpa braced himself, there was a large collision. What could have been a huge disaster, fortunately only resulted in Sgt. Seabold of Company D being thrown overboard and breaking his leg. Grandpa and I both thought it ironic that after surviving sub- infested waters, the only injury to occur was the result of an accident-in France no less! Despite this mishap the rest of the regiment arrived safely on French soil by that afternoon.

It was clear as the men filed through Calais that they, or at least their money, were welcome there. Decorations and signs hung from the shops and homes which read "American Bar", "English spoken", and "American souvenirs." Large groups of French children greeted the men with great enthusiasm shouting the only English they knew, such as, "cigarette for me", "un penny", or oddly, "goodbye". The men continued their march through Calais, soaking in all the new sights and sounds, and didn't stop until they reached their rest camp, one and a half kilometers away.

That night the 119th experienced another new danger- an air raid. It seem the Germans wanted to welcome the Yanks as well, and a German plane flew over dropping several bombs. A lot of noise and confusion resulted, but apparently no one got hurt. The division history records that the men showed "excellent morale" during the attack, but nonetheless began to understand that these shells were "no longer fired by friendly hands in practice", but instead by "enemy craft.... with lethal intent." It was a sobering moment, and it prompted an immediate response. To ensure the men's safety, the next day, the 29th, the division quickly issued order # 13. With the admonition to get the job done "at once", the men were ordered to pitch their tents under trees or alongside hedges, and build 3'x2' embankments around each tent. With all the urgent activities and new dangers occupying his thoughts, I wonder if Grandpa stopped to reflect that his second day in France was also his twenty second birthday.

The regiment stayed in their camp for the next three days. During this time rumors began to circulate that they were to be assigned to the British. As of yet the men didn't know the truth, but as they began to turn in some of their gear they began to figure it out. Campaign hats were exchanged for overseas caps and helmets. Canvas leggings were replaced with British puttees (they were like leggings, only they wrapped around a man's lower legs) and their Springfield rifles were turned in for the British Enfield. Uniformity of weapons and ammunition would allow for more efficiency, and conveniences in supplying the troops of course. But this was small consolation to the "Old Hickory" boys, who grumbled in no small degree the loss of their beloved Springfields. Compared to the perfectly balanced Springfield the Enfield proved to be smaller, clumsier, and awkward.

Army troops at Calais, France, inspecting their British rifles, which replaced the American made Springfield model.

The men quickly discovered that the manual of arms was now

much harder to perform. Despite their discontent, the Enfield would now be the weapon the Thirtieth would fight with the next six months.

Using an unfamiliar weapon was not the only adjustment Grandpa and the others had to make those first few days. They were now in a foreign country that was a far cry from the farms and small towns in Illinois, Tennessee and the Carolinas. There was a language barrier of course, but the men, like any typical tourist picked up a few choice phrases, such as "combine", "tout suite", and voule vous". They learned about French money and food too. Naturally French wines was of particular interest. This didn't go unnoticed by the division history which noted rather tongue-in-cheek, that "the potencies of French wines and liqueurs were given an extensive and thorough study." I'm sure.

French homes and barns were typically used as billets.

After their three days in the rest camp, it was time to move the division to new locations for additional training. They loaded up on the famous French boxcars known as "Hommes 40, Chevaux 8", or simple 40 and 8's. In other words, forty men and eight horses. The trains took the men to Audruicq, a small railway station and after unloading, they marched to a collection of villages known as the "Eperliecques" training areas. One of these small villages was Yeuse, whose barns and old houses would serve as billets for Grandpa and the rest of the battalion. If they were expecting to sleep in beds they were disappointed, as straw on the floor would serve as their bedding for the rest of that summer.

Thus ended the third phase of Grandpa's wartime experiences, and what a phase it was, too! In a brief span of twenty- two days, he saw New York City, ocean liners, the Atlantic Ocean, airplanes, sub attacks, and England and France. For a country boy from a small mid-western town nobody heard of, this must've been heady stuff. Now he was in France, with the ominous boom of distant artillery reminding just how far from home he really was. Did he feel scared? He must've. The sub attack and air raid surely brought home the reality of what he was facing. Was he hopeful perhaps? Maybe through some miracle, the war would end any day, and they could all go home. Did he feel excitement? That's possible. After all, he was participating in a grand historic event, fighting in a just cause that his country believed in. Plus, he was young and invulnerable, participating in the adventure of a lifetime. Perhaps he felt a grim determination, a sort of "let's get this damn thing over with" kind of thing. After all, he was a soldier now who, for the last four months, was focused on nothing but preparing for this moment. While it's always risky to project thoughts and feeling on people, especially from the past, I'd nonetheless bet he felt all of this things. And while I can never know exactly what he felt, I am certain of one thing : Grandpa was on the brink of a life-changing event that would take away his youthful innocence. If innocence can be defined as the lack of knowledge, then Private Rakers was about to get an education about what mankind and himself was capable of. He was about to see both the worst and best in his fellow man. He would find his courage, faith, and endurance tested, and he will emerge with a new hard- earned knowledge about himself, and the world.

Chapter IX

Training With the British

British instructors provided additional training to the inexperienced "doughboys' of the 30th Division.

In February, shortly after the decision had been made to "loan" American divisions to the British, the 2nd Corps was formed for that very purpose. Six, then ten, divisions were originally assigned to it, but eventually it was whittled down to only two: the 27th and 30th Divisions.

The 27th Division, commanded by Major General John Ryan, couldn't have been more different from its counterpart. Unlike the 30th with its country boys, southern roots, and Dixie heritage, the 27th was a "Yankee" organization filled with city boys, factory workers, and immigrants. Whereas the 30th had its Bucks, Otis's, and Orville's filling out it's rosters, the 27th had more foreign names like Max, Epifanio, and

Antonio. However, like the 30[th,] its various National Guard units had also chased Pancho Villa before the war. In addition, the division also received its training in South Carolina at Camp Wadsworth. Before going off to the sunny south, the 27th marched through downtown New York, in what is considered to be one of the largest parades New York has ever seen. Thousands of New Yorkers lined 5th Avenue that August day in 1917, waving flags, shouting hurrahs, and throwing candy, gum, fruit, cigars, and cigarettes to its Yankee warriors. As fate would have it, the destiny of both divisions would become deeply intertwined in the months ahead.

Once in France, the 2nd Corps would take its place in the British sector and be under British command. Because they were now serving with the "Tommies", there would be a need for uniformity of arms, equipment and rations. In other words Grandpa would wear a British helmet, fire a British rifle, and eat British food. British rations would include meat, cheese, tea, and the detested marmalade. Needless to say, the doughboys were quite disgruntled with their culinary prospects. However, General Simonds, Chief of Staff of the 2nd Corps, came to the rescue, convincing the British to make some changes, such as coffee for tea, and increasing the quantities of other rations. Nothing was said about the marmalade.

As per the agreement made in February, the soldiers of the 2nd corps were to receive additional training from British officers and non-coms. The training was designed to unfold in two phases, A and B. While the 30th overall would receive instruction from the British 39th Division, the 119th Regiment would be taught by a cadre of instructors from the 9th Black Watch and the 9th and 10th Gordon Highlanders. Phase A ran through June and much of July. The men received additional training on the Lewis Gun, musketry, bombing, bayonet fighting, scouting, sniping, and gas training. Time was also devoted to march discipline and trench warfare. During this period Field Marshall Douglas Haig (Commander of the British armies in France), and General Pershing inspected the 119th Regiment. Both went away extremely pleased with what they saw. Pershing, in particular, commented that he had not seen a better body of men in the entire A.E.F.

Haig and Pershing were not the only special guests that the division received that summer. As the divisional history described it, on August 6th King George V and a "galaxy" of high ranking British and American officials arrived to inspect the men. He didn't stay long. After a quick inspection of only the front ranks, he gave a "snappy" salute before jumping into his car and leaving as quickly as he arrived. However, previously on July 23rd, the division received a guest who would stay a little longer. Her name was Elsie Janis, and she was the "Sweetheart of the A.E.F."!

Few people today have heard of Elsie Janis, but in Grandpa's day, she was a very popular comedic star. She began her career in Vaudeville at the tender age of two, and by the time she was eleven she was a Vaudeville headliner. In time she also became a headliner on both Broadway and the London stage, enjoying the acclaim of both American and British critics. When the war broke out she took her act on the road, and pre-dating Bob Hope by twenty-five years, became one of the first American performers to entertain troops overseas. She performed in all kinds of conditions; it didn't matter. She would do her act from the back of a truck, on top of a table, or in the middle of the road. She would perform in the camps and hospitals. Mud and rain did not deter her as she tried to perform as many times as she could in the course of a day. In performances described as gutsy, touching, and patriotic, she would shout out her customary greeting *Are we downhearted? No!"* She could do it all. She would sing and tell jokes. She would do imitations of the popular performers of the day, like Eddie Foy, Sarah Bernhardt, Will Rogers, and Ethel Barrymore. Finally she would end her act with a rousing performance as George M. Cohan, singing "Over There".

Phase B of their training began on July 2nd when the division started a three day march to Belgium and the front. It was extremely hot that summer morning when the 119th regiment formed up on the Zaufques-Louchs-Yeuse Road. In full field packs the men took their place on the road and at 9:45 began their march. Grandpa had to carry 120 rounds of ammunition, one cooked meal, full field equipment, and a blanket. It must've been quite a sight as thousands of men in their wool uniforms marched and sweated in the Belgian heat, kicking up choking clouds of dust. Adding to the scene were numerous horse drawn wagons of various descriptions; sanitation wagons, rolling kitchens, baggage wagons, water carts, and limbers all contributed to the clamor of the march.

By the end of the day the regiment had marched roughly eight to nine miles before setting up camp. Their rest was short- livcd though, as they were up early the next morning, and re-formed by 6:15 to continue the march. They covered another eight to ten miles by days end and camped that night in a local pasture. The next day was the Fourth of July, and as the Division continued its march it had the honor of being the "first to plant foot on Belgian soil" as the divisional history proudly recorded. Celebrating its arrival and our national holiday, Belgians lined the route waving cheerful greetings and waving American flags. That night the 119th regiment made camp in Herzeele. It was here that the men first heard the firing of the guns on the famous Flanders front, and it was the cause for much discussion. As indeed it should have been.

Flanders had been the setting for some of the worst fighting on the Western front with five major battles fought at Ypres in 1914, 1915, 1916, 1917, and again in 1918. The ghastly four month battle of the Somme, with its 58,000 casualties on the first day alone, was also fought in this region. These were battles that were characterized by the first use of poison gas, tanks, flamethrowers, and mud so liquid that wounded men were known to disappear in it. It was the killing fields of Flanders that inspired doomed Canadian John McCrae to pen the poem *In Flanders Fields*, with its images of red poppies growing between crosses "row on row". And it was the fighting in Flanders that ultimately took over 1,700,000 combined casualties by wars end. Yeah, they should've been talking about it. They were sitting near a charnel house, and it wouldn't be long before the young men of the 30th would shed their blood in Flanders Field too.

The division was given a four day rest before they resumed phase B of their training. Yet it must have been a rest tinged with anxiety. They were extremely close to the fighting now, with their closest point only twelve kilometers from the front. As they went about their duties, their day was punctuated with the thunder of distant artillery. Nightfall failed to provide any relief, as air raids occurred almost every night, hitting crossroads and camps. Wagons hauling rations to the front were favorite targets of the Germans, and on several occasions the division H.Q. at Watou was shelled. If the green doughboys had any doubts they were in a war zone, the shelling and bombing had to have convinced them otherwise.

Now that the division was close to the front they were ready to complete phase B of their training. From July 16th to August 10th the division would begin to take its place in the trenches and experience front line conditions. This would be the final step before being committed to actual combat. In its usual crisp, authoritative fashion, the divisional history describes how this experience would unfold. Over a period of weeks, groups of men, small at first and then gradually larger, would be rotated in and out of the trench systems for extended periods of time. The experience would unfold over three periods, and be conducted under the watchful eyes of their British mentors. Groups of non-coms and selected enlisted men attached to the British units would go in first for a forty-eight hour rotation. Then, in the second period, platoons of a given battalion were attached as platoons to British companies for a four day stretch. Finally, in the third period each of the three battalions of a regiment would relieve a British battalion for an eight day period. No more than one battalion would serve at the front at a time. The remaining two battalions would serve in the reserve trenches that supported the main line. For example, the third battalion, which was Grandpa's, occupied the reserve trench until August 1st. Then under the cover of darkness (all movements took place at night) it relieved the second battalion, and took its place in the line.

The Thirtieth Division in line; Canal Sector, Ypres-Lys.

To help the frightened, green doughboys adjust to life in the trenches, a quiet sector was usually picked for this experience. However this didn't prove to be the case for the 30th. As a German attack on their position was anticipated, British artillery kept up a steady shelling on any perceived enemy movements. Naturally the Germans returned the favor, and what should have been a relatively quiet sector quickly became very hot. It didn't take long before the division began to take casualties. The 119th in particular was hit hard. In an eighteen day period between July 23rd and August 10th the regiment lost forty two men. Between August 4th and 6th, Grandpa's Company K lost three men to the shelling. The period of August 2nd through the 9th proved to be particularly bloody, as Company I lost a total of twelve men; eight of them killed on the 2nd alone. The regimental history dryly noted that "casualties numbered more than was expected."

Orville gives us a sense of what that experience was like in his *World War I Remembered*. Making their way on a dirt road to the front, they would pass the men they were relieving. As their comrades passed them by, Orville couldn't help noticing how "dirty and tired" they looked. The sounds of the war with its big cannons and gunfire became louder as they got closer, and with it came a growing sense of dread. "It was very difficult as we really didn't know what to expect", he said. The whistle of a shell would send the men diving into a ditch for cover, and when they stopped to rest they dug fox holes for protection. "It's impossible to describe how you felt at that time", he said, "not knowing what to expect, and realizing that the next shell could kill you." Life in the trenches was hardly better. The roar of the big guns, the whistle of shells zipping overhead, and the deafening explosions continued unabated. The day to day living in the trenches was miserable. Its muddy, wet conditions, Orville said, left the men "cold and unable to rest." After a week the men would be relieved, and they would rotate to the rear for some badly needed rest. Yet as Orville noted, this only made the return to the front all the more difficult, "because now we knew what to expect."

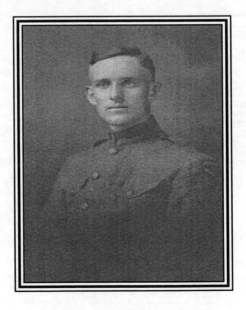

Private Orville Hinton

Upon completion of phase B, the division was withdrawn to the rear and out of danger from enemy shellfire. Here they briefly rested and fine-tuned their training. For all practical purposes the men of the 30th were now "graduates" of their training, and ready to take their place in battle. The divisional history proudly noted that the men were now "efficient", "highly motivated", and "eager and ready" to fight alongside their allies. It wouldn't be long before Grandpa and the rest would fight in the great offensive they had been trained for, and break the Hindenburg Line.

On August 16th, following a brief rest, the division received new orders. Under the cover of darkness they were moved to the front lines at the Canal sector near Ypres. Here they were to relieve the battered veterans of the British 33rd Division, and for the first time, take their place in the lines-alone. This would be the beginning of a six week tour of duty, with the 30th rotating in and out of the front lines. Here the men would learn how to endure life in the trenches, with all its attendant hardships and miseries. This would be Grandpa's baptism of fire, as he and the division would experience, for the first time, the excitement and terror of combat. And at the end of this difficult six weeks, the division would emerge as battle-tested veterans, whose ultimate task laid just before them.

Chapter X

Life In The Trenches!

Standing in water and mud was just several of the many hardships the men had to endure, living in the trenches. (Courtesy of National World War I Museum, Kansas City, Mo.)

Somehow the divisional history with its sanitized account of the 30th's introduction to the trenches fails to communicate the harsh reality of that experience. Its account is typical military speak with its bare bones description of "efficient", "eager", and "well trained" men ready to charge into the fray. Not only is the divisional history guilty of this, but Grandpa, despite his many trench tales, never did communicate to me just how horrible life in the trenches was either. He would give me glimpses of it, often with a humorous tale, or maybe something a little grimmer, but he spared me the true ugliness of it. And that is the nub of the matter. How could he tell his children and grandchildren the awful reality of trench life?

By the time the 30th arrived in Belgium, the trenches that so characterized the Great War were well in place. Stretching from the Alps to the North Sea, over four hundred miles of trenches was home to millions of English, German, and French soldiers. Try to imagine that. That's a continuous ditch dug across the state of Missouri from Kansas City to just beyond St. Louis. While there were variations in the particulars in different trench systems (German trenches were more elaborate for example) they basically followed the same design. Both sides built their trenches with an emphasis on concealing and protecting their men. As much as possible trenches were dug to be five feet– deep about the height of an average man- so that he wouldn't be exposed to enemy fire. For further protection they were kept as narrow as possible, yet wide enough for two men to pass. They were built in a zig zag pattern to minimize the damage of a direct hit from a shell, or an enemy firing down its length. The trenches were constantly muddy and in danger of caving in. To try and cope with these ever present problems plank flooring called "duckboards" were put into place, and the walls were reinforced with burlap sandbags. So the soldiers could repel an attack, fire steps were built along the length of the trench.

Behind the front trench were the so called "communication trenches" that ran perpendicular to the front trench. These trenches linked the front line trench to the support and reserve trenches that ran parallel to the front. Through these trenches men, food, water, ammo, and supplies could be brought to the front and the wounded, sick, and dead to the rear. Located throughout the trench system would be dugouts carved into the sides, and even underneath the trench. These would serve as first aid stations, store rooms, HQ, sleeping quarters, and bomb shelters. Of course there were latrines, whose offensive odor only added to the already suffocating stench. But more on that later.

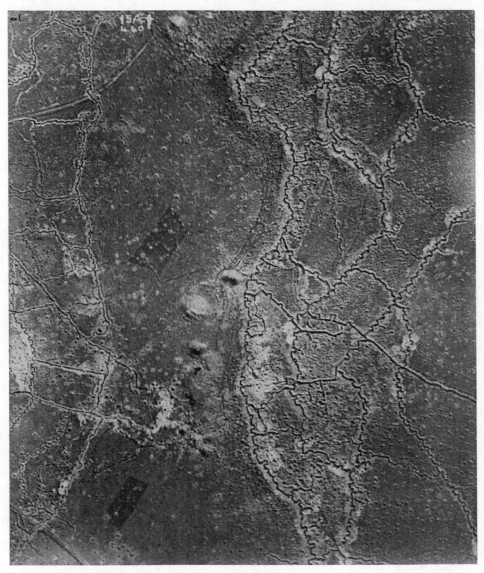

This aerial photograph shows British and German trenches. Note "No man's land" and the countless shell holes.

(Courtesy of National World War I Museum. Kansas City, Missouri.)

Laying between the opposing trenches was a terrain that has often been described as a lunar landscape. Pockmarked with countless shell holes, uprooted trees, and acres and acres of barbed wire it was known simply as "no man's land". Aptly named, these open spaces between the trenches were nothing more than killing fields. With the screech of whistles signaling the assault, attacks would begin with thousands of men clambering out of the safety of the trench, and charging as best they could across open ground. Shell holes, barbed wire, and the ubiquitous mud would slow the attack down, making them easy targets. The enemy, safely hidden in his trenches and heavily armed with machine guns and artillery, would simply mow them down like wheat before a scythe. Very few attacks succeeded, and what success was achieved was often measured in yards.

Surviving an attack was only one challenge soldiers of WWI had to face. The other more prevailing struggle was enduring the daily grind of trench life. Boredom, water and mud, lice, rats, lousy food, and the unbelievable stench all conspired to make these men as miserable as can be imagined. It's a wonder they didn't all go mad.

Probably the first thing that greeted Grandpa when he took his place in the trenches was the overwhelming stink. It would've been a nauseating mix of competing odors that instantly assaulted the senses. Perhaps he gagged or threw up. Many a doughboy making their first visit to the reeking trenches did just that. A discriminating nose would've immediately picked out the wet rotting burlap sandbags bolstering the walls. There would've been the foul smell of standing stagnant water. The men themselves, unwashed, often for weeks and wearing sweaty filthy uniforms, added to the funk. The smell of cordite from exploded shells, or the sickeningly sweet lingering aroma of an old gas attack contributed to the reek. The latrines with their repulsive sewer-like stink added to the all-pervasive stench, even more so when struck by a direct hit. Finally there were the dead. Vicious battles left no-man's land and the trenches littered with the dead and dying. If it was possible, the dead were buried, but this often proved futile as artillery barrages would only churn up the putrid corpses. Of course recovering the dead from no-man's land was impossible. So the dead would rot under the sun while the next breeze would send the sickening smell back to the trenches. The smell alone would've been enough to test the fortitude of any man, but tragically there was more.

There were other occupants living in the trenches besides the men: rats and lice. Grandpa never did speak of rats, and it's probably just as well, given how disgusting it was. Rats can reproduce prodigiously and it didn't take long before millions inhabited the trenches, getting into the food stores and spreading infection. Armies were never able to come to terms with them. Often feeding on the dead, they could grow into the size of house cats. Naturally the men feared and despised them. It was bad enough to see them skittering across the trench floor in broad daylight, but it was horrible to be awakened by one scampering across your face in the middle of the night. The men clubbed them, shot them, and bayoneted them, but in the end never could eliminate them. All they could do was endure them. Despite their repulsiveness some soldiers claimed there was one benefit. Many veterans swore that rats could sense impending enemy barrages, and would disappear accordingly, providing an early warning system.

While Grandpa never spoke to me about rats, he did talk about lice, the bane of soldier's existence since the day of Roman Legionnaires. Living in the muck and mire of the trenches, and with no means for washing themselves or their uniforms, the men became lousy. The lice, or cooties as they were called, would breed in the seams of uniforms, and cause the men to itch incessantly. While the itching was maddening enough, the lice presented the bigger problem of disease. Lice caused "trench fever", a painful disease that would begin with severe pain followed by a high fever. It could take up to twelve weeks to recover. Virtually impossible to eradicate, there were nonetheless periodic attempts to cleanse the men and their uniforms with delousing stations, something Grandpa did speak of. But in the end they never could completely get rid of them, try as they might. Once, in desperation I suppose, Grandpa took his infested sweater that had been a gift from some Oconee women, and whipped it around a post in a barn trying to knock them out, but to no avail. And then there was the mud. Throughout time wars have been fought in many hellish settings, but one would be hard pressed to find one worse than Flanders in WWI. Due to the fortunes of war it was the British, French and Americans' who would languish and suffer in the mud the most. Following the Battle of the Marne in 1914, the Germans had been forced to fall back as far as the Aisne River. Determined not to lose any further ground, the Germans began to dig in and prepare defensive positions. Thus the trench system began with the Germans possessing a critical advantage. They were able to dig in on the ground of their own choosing, and predictably chose the higher ground. The French and British, on the other hand, had no choice but to dig in at the lower elevations. It would be these simple military maneuvers, along with geography that would ultimately make the mud of the western front such a miserable feature of the war.

The plains of Flanders is low and swampy, with much of it barely above sea level. A system of several rivers and an extensive drainage system crisscrossed its terrain. These factors, along with its clay and sandy soil did not make it an ideal setting for trenches. Men couldn't dig too deep without hitting water. When it rained, and it rained a lot, the water could not pass through the dense clay soil. Plus the constant artillery barrages soon smashed the drainage systems, making conditions worse. In short order the trenches became a water logged, muddy, gooey, mess. As a result, the men were always wet and caked with mud. It seems hard to believe, but there are stories of men becoming so stuck in the mud that they literally had to use their hands to pull their feet out. Grimmer yet, there are tales of horses dying from exhaustion as they tried to fight their way out of the muck, or of men too weak to save themselves, drowning in the morass. It became so bad that the hospitals became crowded with men suffering for a malady called "trench foot".

Did you ever have the experience as a child of being in the bath water too long? You probably noticed how your fingers and toes began to wrinkle and shrivel up. That is, to a lesser degree, trench foot. The water- logged conditions of the trenches forced men to stand in water for hours on end without the benefit of removing their soaked shoes and socks. In time a man's feet will become numb, and if there is poor circulation, his feet will turn either red or blue. His feet will begin to put out a decaying odor as they begin to rot, and if left untreated for too long, will begin to swell. If not treated immediately, gangrene will set in, often leading to amputation. However, if treated quickly and properly, a man could regain the normal use of his feet, although his recovery would be marked by severe short term pain, as feeling returned.

Grandpa was hospitalized twice for trench foot, although when it happened is unclear. In any case, he once described to me how on one occasion his leg began to swell up, and became covered with black and blue spots. He reported to sick call and the doctor sent him to a British field hospital in Bolounge France, where he spent the next three weeks recovering. Interestingly, three years after the war on March 30th, 1921, Grandpa filed an insurance claim with the Federal government. In that document Grandpa declared that his military service had left him afflicted with rheumatism and flat feet. Was this a lingering effect of his bout with trench foot? I can't say, but it demonstrates, I think, the terrible conditions of trench life that Grandpa suffered. Like so many doughboys, the war and life in the trenches would leave its mark on the men both physically and emotionally. How could it not? What Grandpa experienced in the trenches must've been awful. Is it any wonder he didn't tell more?

Chapter XI

War Stories

Bolougne, France, 1918. Grandpa wears a Scottish uniform after some fun in town.

Despite his reticence about life in the trenches, Grandpa was nonetheless a natural story teller. I can still see him sitting at the head of the dinner table telling us yet another story about the farm or the war. It wasn't unusual for him to repeat a story more than once though, and there were several that were standards Grandpa would trot out whenever the family was together. I don't know if it was because he was forgetful, or if he just liked telling them, but it didn't matter to me. I loved hearing them, and enjoyed them every time.

Whenever possible, I have tried to place Grandpa's stories within a larger context to give his anecdotes more meaning. I have also tried as much as I can, to pinpoint in time when these stories occurred, but it has not always been possible. The destruction of his personal file, which no doubt would've helped immensely, has been lamented many times in the course of this writing. So unfortunately, some of his stories just kind of hang out there in space as it were, lacking an anchor in time. However, given the fact that many of his stories occurred in battle, the trenches, or in the hospital, it's safe to say they would've occurred during the late summer and autumn months of 1918. Also, as I think about it, most of Grandpa's stories were about food, illness, or battle. Shouldn't surprise me I guess; as far as war is concerned, what else is there?

One time when they were in the trenches, an officer ordered Grandpa to prepare his dinner. Included in the menu was a tomato. Officers, with their special privileges, Grandpa explained, could buy extra groceries to supplement their mundane army rations. Enlisted men, of course, could not. Grandpa had not seen a tomato since he left the states, and as he looked at it he must've wondered at the injustice of it all. It didn't take long for him to make a decision though-he ate it! Shortly afterwards he dutifully delivered the meal and left. It wasn't long, he said, before he was summoned before the aggrieved officer.

"Private Rakers!" the officer barked.
"Yes sir!" Grandpa answered.
"Was there a tomato with my dinner?"
"Yes sir!" Grandpa answered.

"Where is it??"

I ate it sir!" And every time Grandpa told this story, he would heartily laugh at the memory of his insubordination. "What could they do to me?" He would say, "I was already at the front!"

Other food stories weren't so funny. My mother remembers his telling about eating his breakfast of oatmeal in the rain. Of course it got soggier and soggier, but he managed to choke it down somehow. The memory of it never left him, and he didn't touch another bowl of oatmeal again until he was an old man. He also told another story, a simple one really about how hungry a man can get. They had been at the front for a long time, and were finally relieved, and given a chance to retire to a rest camp for a much needed break. As they wearily trudged their way back to the rear, they passed through a small town that had a small restaurant. A long line of doughboys waited in line to get a meal. A very hungry Grandpa took his place with them. Once inside, he ordered a dozen fried eggs, over easy with all the trimmings. Try eating a dozen fried eggs sometime.

Finally, there was this odd story Grandpa told me several times. He and a sergeant once came upon the corpse of a German soldier. The sergeant encouraged Grandpa to search his field pack to see what he could find. Grandpa obliged and proceeded to roll the body over, unbuckle the straps, and search its contents. He pulled out a loaf of black bread, and not surprisingly, took a bite. Expecting a tasty morsel, he was disappointed and disgusted, as the bread, he said, "became slicker and slicker" the more he chewed. Now, I never knew exactly what he meant by that, and I'm not sure I want to know, (worms no doubt) but it was obvious to me that moment made a lasting impression on him. And the funny thing was, after he spat out the bread, Grandpa methodically placed the loaf back in the pack, buckled it up, and rolled the dead German back over, leaving him just the way he found him. Grandpa would chuckle at the irony of that.

As previously noted, Grandpa had two hospital stays during the war, which provided both terrifying and humorous experiences. During one stay-it's not clear which – Grandpa laid asleep in his bed.

Suddenly he became aware that somebody was suffocating him with a pillow. Gasping for air, he began to struggle, when suddenly he heard a female voice telling him to relax; there was nothing to fear. The Germans were shelling the town, the voice said, and the nurses were putting pillows over the patient's faces to protect them from flying glass. So Grandpa laid there, explosions punctuating the air, waiting for the danger to pass.

It was during his second visit Grandpa laid next to a wounded seventeen- year- old English soldier. He had thirteen shrapnel wounds on him, Grandpa said. When the nurse came by to check their temperatures, she placed thermometers in their mouths, and gave them each a cup of hot cocoa. Perhaps feeling some sympathy for Grandpa, the English lad prodded Grandpa to put his thermometer in the hot cocoa. A high temperature could keep him away from the front after all! Given Grandpa's penchant for mischief, you'd think he would've done it, but he didn't, or so he said.

One of the memories Grandpa had of these hospital stays were his visits to a nearby beach. That's all he ever said of it really, and it seems like such a simple story. But I think there's more to it than he let on. The hospital Grandpa was placed in was a British field hospital in Boulogne, France. Boulogne is an ancient French coastal city not far from Calais, and there are beaches nearby. It not clear to me how he would get there, but whenever he could he would go to the beach to watch the people swimming. To my knowledge that's all he ever said of it, but I imagine those visits meant a lot to him. It would have been quiet and peaceful, with only the sounds of the waves, and happy people. The war would've been far away, and he could forget it for a while. It would've been good for his soul.

And then there was this story, my favorite. During one of his hospital stays word came down that all of the walking wounded had to leave the hospital. A big offensive was coming, and room had to be made in the hospital for the new wounded. Accordingly, Grandpa and the other walking wounded were transferred to a rest camp. It was there that Grandpa became acquainted with a twenty three year

114

old Scottish Sergeant, who had been the assistant postmaster in Glasgow, Scotland before the war. They got chummy, and finally the sergeant suggested they go to Boulogne and have a little fun. When Grandpa protested that he didn't have a pass, his new friend reminded him he was a sergeant and that, "The guards won't see us go by." Persuaded, Grandpa followed his new pal to the gates. As the two approached the guards, the Sergeant instructed Grandpa "don't look at 'em, and just keep walking." It worked. Soon they were in Boulogne looking for a bank to get some cash. Seems as if the sergeant was broke and Grandpa was "paying the way!" The British didn't get paid much, Grandpa explained, and he had $50 which he exchanged for French francs. After leaving the bank they promptly bought a bottle of whiskey and searched out a restaurant. Grandpa remembered that as they sat there enjoying their meal and drinks, people would walk by, and laugh at the site of a doughboy and a tommy enjoying themselves.

Done eating, the two of them headed back to the hospital to visit the wounded. Then one of them, Grandpa didn't say who, got an idea. A photographic studio was nearby, and the two of them decided to go back and have their photographs taken-*in each other's uniform*! So Grandpa donned this buddy's tunic, plaid kilt, and bonnet, and posed for his picture looking every bit the part of a Scottish soldier in the King's army. It would be an appropriate souvenir of their day. It was getting late and they needed to get back to camp before the sun set, but not before they bought a bottle of champagne to drink on the way. Posing for pictures can make a soldier thirsty, I guess.

The next day there was trouble. Both men were summoned before the camps commanding officer, who informed them, "They had been missed!" Both soldiers pled guilty to being absent without leave (AWOL), but apparently there would be no disciplinary action taken. There was an offensive about to begin, and both would be needed by their units. The commanding officer probably figured that if they were well enough to party in town, they were well enough to go back to the war. Which, I would imagine, would've been punishment enough. The following day, both found themselves on trucks going off in different directions, and in twenty- four hours Grandpa was back on the firing line. He never saw the sergeant again.

Many years later Grandpa told me that story, and gave me that photo. I prize that picture and it hangs proudly on my wall. I look at it often, and when I do, I can't help but wonder if there is some family in Scotland today, with a similar picture of their soldier boy in a doughboy's uniform. Wouldn't you love to see that picture too?

Chapter XII

The YPres–Lyes Offensive

Kemmel Hill at the Ypres Salient

From the time Grandpa trained in South Carolina, to the division's assignment to the canal sector, dramatic events had been unfolding on the western front that would ultimately shape the final outcome of the war. In that 5-6 month period, as the U.S. desperately tried to get armies to France before it was too late, Germany launched the so called "spring offensives." There were five offensives in all, and it was Germany's last-ditch effort to win the war before the growing American presence tipped the balance forever out of reach. Much to everyone's shock, they almost succeeded.

Between March 21st and July 15th 1918 the Germans, using their new "Storm trooper" tactics, launched five hammer blow attacks on the allies. The British never saw the first attack coming.

The Village of Voormezeele, Belgium, September 1, 1918.
Captured by the Thirtieth Division.

Opening the attack with a barrage of 6.473 guns the British were sent reeling back in panicked retreat. However, despite a German breakthrough and the collapse of the British 5th army, the attack was eventually blunted and absolute disaster averted. Yet, in the following attacks of April and May (when the 30th arrived in France), the Germans were able to smash through French defenses, advance thirty five miles, capture 65, 000 prisoners, and come within thirty seven miles of Paris. The situation was desperate, to say the least.

Despite the A.E.F.'s relative small numbers at this point, and their lack of experience, General Pershing offered two divisions to the French in their attempt to counter attack, and blunt the German juggernaut. The resulting battles at Cantigny (May 28th), Chateau-Thierry (May 31st), and Belleau Woods (June 1st and 26th) would be the A.E.F.'s baptism of fire. Despite incurring terrific casualties, it played a key role in helping stop the German advance and turn the tide. Any reading about America's role in WW I will inevitably cover these battles.

The last German offensive took place on July 15th, and had sputtered out by the 17th. Germany had gambled one last time and lost. Like two boxers in the ring, Germany had delivered its best punches to an opponent who was able to absorb incredible punishment. Exhausted, she waited for her opponent to come back swinging. She wouldn't have long to wait.

While Grandpa was nowhere near this action when it occurred, his cousin John Rakers was. When we last heard of John, he had shipped out with his contingent from Shelbyville for infantry training and assignment to the 39th Infantry. John claimed he was the second best shot in his company, so he was made the trigger man of a three-man machine gun crew. (My guess it was the French-made Hotchkiss machine gun, which was operated by three men: one to fire and two to load). In due course, he found himself in France, and in late May, 1918, he was in the "thick of it" at Chouteau-Thierry. One day while advancing down a road, a shell exploded in front of his company. Reflexively, he tried to dodge the blast by jumping down an adjacent hill. He successfully avoided the blast, but managed to seriously injure his arm in the fall. It was his lucky day. He had sustained what future generations of soldiers would call "a million dollar wound". While he would remain in the army for the duration of the war, his disability kept him out of any further fighting.

After his fall he was taken to a first aid station and eventually to a field hospital. As he was taken to his bed, the attendants checked his dog tags, and noticed his name was Rakers. They informed him that earlier that morning another soldier named Rakers had died in that same bed. Naturally John wondered aloud if it was his Oconee cousin. They didn't know. It wouldn't be until after the war was over, when he was back home, that he would learn that his cousin had survived the war.

John spent the rest of the war guarding German P.O.W.s. He

claimed he didn't have to work too hard because the prisoners never had it so good. They were out of the war and they had plenty to eat, such as coffee and doughnuts. Hell, they weren't going anywhere. He remembered how the prisoners loved to sing, especially at Christmas when "Silent Night" could be heard all across the camps. He remembered the constant rumble of the distant guns leading up to November 11th, and the deafening silence following the armistice. Finally, he recalled how he got deathly ill, as millions did at the end of the war. He had fallen victim to the great influenza outbreak that ultimately killed more people than the war ever did. There were so many deaths he said, that the camp had twelve grave diggers working around the clock. He himself was in a coma for four days before he finally recovered, but not before his own grave had also been dug!

John would survive the war, and go back home to Oconee where he would live out the remainder of his days. In 1992, four years after I interviewed him, John died at the age of ninety- nine.

Following the failures of the spring offensives, it was the Allies' turn to launch attacks of their own. The defeat of the German offensives, and the presence of a two million man American army, convinced French Generalissimo Ferdinand Foch (commander-in-chief of the allied armies), the time was right to make a final push to end this bloody mess once and for all. Starting with the Battle of Amien on August 8th, to the Armistice on November 11th, the Allies would engage in what became known as the "Hundred day's offensive." Despite its misleading name, it wasn't a single battle, but instead it was an almost unbroken series of bloody fights that would push the German army back to their last lines of defense, the Hindenburg Line. It would be here, at the Hindenburg Line, where the allies would mass for one final push. Once they broke the line, it was only a matter of time before the war would be over.

The Battle of Amiens, on August 8th, 1918 marked the beginning of this period. Ten allied divisions of British, Australian, Canadian, and French troops managed to completely surprise the Germans and smash through their lines. Armed with 500 tanks, a fifteen- mile gap was blasted in the German lines, and by the tenth, the allies had penetrated twelve miles into the German positions. The German army was forced to fall back the same day, and retreat towards the Hindenburg Line. When it was all over, the German's had lost 17,000 prisoners, 330 guns, and 30,000 killed or wounded. German morale was collapsing, and it was, as General Erich Ludendorff (the chief manager of the German war effort) would later write, "The black day of the German army." It is said, that Ludendorff was so distraught over the defeats, he had a massive, Teutonic, temper tantrum in front of his staff! Throughout the rest of August and early September, the allies would fight numerous battles as they tried to eliminate salients (more on that later) and drive the Germans back, to better position themselves for the upcoming contest.

It was in this cauldron of violence that Grandpa would first experience combat.

As mentioned earlier, on August 16th the division was sent to what was known as the Canal Sector of the Ypres Salient. Their mission was to assist the British in driving the Germans from this position. Known as the Ypres-Lys offensive, it was one of those seemingly endless engagements that made up the "Hundred Days offensive". To better understand what will follow, it is necessary to talk about salients, and their role on the Western Front.

Try to imagine a long continuous line running from point A to point B, with opposing armies occupying each side of the line. Imagine that one of these armies, in its attempt to push the enemy back, bends a portion of the line forming a bulge. That bulge, (Perhaps you have heard of the "Battle of the Bulge" in WWII?) in military terms, is called a salient. The technical definition for this feature is "an area of the battle field that extends into enemy territory and is surrounded on three sides." The problem salients create for the occupying army, is that they are surrounded on three sides, making them very vulnerable to enemy fire. If the salient penetrates too deeply into enemy lines, it has the added danger of possibly being "pinched out" across its base, thereby completing its encirclement. The troops inside this "pocket" are then trapped and cut off. In time, without reinforcements or supplies, it simply becomes overrun. By 1918 there were a number of these bulges or salients up and down the Western Front. The largest and most deadly of these, was the Ypres-Lys salient in Flanders-exactly where the 30th Division had been assigned.

It was the opening battles of 1914 that first created the Ypres Salient. Although the boundaries of the salient fluctuated some over the years as a result of four offensives prior to 1918 (three German, one British), the bulge in the line remained essentially the same. A popular description of the time likened it to a saucer, with the Germans occupying the rim or high ground that encircled the salient to the North, East, and South. Occupying the center of the saucer, where the cup would sit, was the ancient city of Ypres, famous for its textile industry and magnificent 13th century Cloth Hall. Its location made it vulnerable to almost constant shelling by German artillery, and within short order the town, including Cloth Hall, was in ruins. Despite its dangerous location, the British would hold onto Ypres for the duration of the war.

The strategic importance of the Ypres Salient would make it the setting for some of the fiercest fighting of the war. If the Germans could force their way through the town they would have access to Belgian and French ports and their shipping lanes. Control of these vital ports would allow Germany to block men and materials crossing the English Channel to the front. And in a nightmare scenario no one wanted to contemplate, if the Germans could base U-Boats in those ports, it would be an unthinkable disaster. Ypres also became an important symbol of defiance to the Belgian people. Most of Belgium had been overrun by the German army in 1914, and Ypres and the surrounding Flanders region, was the last piece of Belgian land still under their control. That, and the enormous sacrifices in blood defending Ypres against overwhelming odds, made the Belgians and British determined to hold onto it at all costs. And hold onto it they did, sometimes barely, making the salient as Winston Groom wrote in *A Storm in Flanders*, a "gigantic corpse factory." Grandpa, had indeed been sent to a very dangerous place.

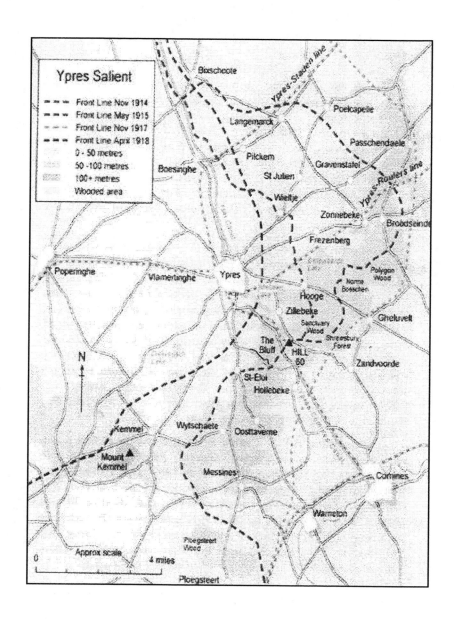

The Canal Sector, to which the 30th had been assigned, laid just southeast of Ypres. Running through the sector was the Ypres-Comines Canal, hence the name of the sector. The surrounding landscape was classic Flanders, with the terrain described by the regimental history as "very low and wet, thus causing many hardships upon the troops." In a letter home, Private Jack Bivins, who was part of the fourth contingent from Shelbyville, wrote "...the Flanders mud is all that they say it is, believe me. *It is the stickiest darn stuff I ever saw!"* He also described a Belgian countryside that had been devastated by almost four years of war with "...Villages razed, ground torn up, great shell holes everywhere." To the left of the sector were the ruins of Ypres. To the far right of it, situated in the highland ridges that formed the "saucer rim" was Kemmel Hill.

Occupied by the Germans, it gave them a commanding view of the whole sector, making it too risky for the British to move about during the day. To offer some protection from enemy fire, camouflaged netting was erected along the main roads leading to the front. However, its protection was spotty at best. Given the nature of the salient, the men often fell victim to enemy shellfire from the front, flanks, and rear. In the *Official History of the 120th Infantry*, it states that sometimes the men in forward positions thought they were being shelled by their own artillery, when in fact it came from the enemy. Perhaps this was the setting for another of Grandpa's stories. Once, he and another soldier had been sent on a detail to bring back boxes of oatmeal for the men's breakfast. Suddenly, they heard the piercing whistle, and felt the hot breath of an incoming shell. Both men instantly dropped the box they were carrying and dove for cover. And, as Grandpa liked to say, as far as he knew, that box of oatmeal is still there today.

On August 19th, several days after the Division took its place in the line, the Ypres-Lys offensive began. On that day and the next, the 30th conducted patrols to try and capture some prisoners. The resulting firefight would give Grandpa his "baptism of fire". A report submitted by Major W.S. Privott of the 3rd Battalion, 119th Infantry (Grandpas' units) described the fight.

"...they occupied dugouts by day but at night would move about rather rapidly, and kept up almost a constant harassing fire...the enemy dugouts were in most cases within 150-250 yards of our outposts. Patrolling by us was extremely difficult on account of such a tangled mass of wire, hedges, and ruins of wrecked fright cars and huts, all of which afforded him good shelter..."

On August 20th the patrols were ordered to fall back to allow British artillery to pound the enemy positions, which the division history described as "...uncomfortably close to our lines." The barrage achieved its desired effect and the patrols resumed their prior positions. Before proceeding any further, however, it was decided by HQ to launch its first gas attack. A horrible weapon, gas had been first used by the Germans at the 2nd Battle of Ypres in 1915. While initially devastating, the armies quickly adapted, and began to equip themselves with gas masks to protect themselves. Before long, all of the armies began to use poison gas.

Weather conditions were critical to the success of a gas attack. In other words, there had to be enough wind, and it had to be blowing the right way! For this upcoming attack, the orders issued by HQ, required a wind velocity of no less than four miles per hour, and a wind direction between north and west. August 26th and 27th 1918 met those conditions. To prepare for the attack it took, according to the divisional history, nine trains of seven cars each, to haul 2,550 gas cylinders weighing a total of 120 tons. The gas cylinders were pushed into position by 11:30 the night of the 26th and at 2:25 the following morning, the gas was released. As it turned out, it was a lot of work for very little result.

The divisional history is rather terse about what happened next, but apparently the wind shifted and the gas blew back towards the American lines. Men began to run, but wire entanglements interfered "...with the progress of men seeking a point of safety." Several men of Company F of the engineers, became casualties of their own attack. As far as the enemy were concerned, according to some prisoners, the only casualties they experienced were the loss of some animals.

Meanwhile, on the 26th, the same day the gas attack was to begin, HQ issued orders for the 60th brigade to be relieved from the line by the 59th Brigade. However, events on the German side of the line would prevent this from happening, and would set the stage for additional fighting.

Following the Battle of Amiens, and the British and French offensives south of Ypres, the German's began a slow withdrawal towards the Hindenburg Line. To assist in their defense, additional troops were pulled out from the Ypres-Lys region and sent south to bolster German forces there. Faced with having fewer troops in the sector the German's had to shorten their lines which meant evacuating Kemmel Hill. They established a new line at the Wytschete-Messines Ridge located approximately seven kilometers southeast of Kemmel Hill. But, to hold the British in check and not reveal their withdrawal, machine gun posts were positioned across the hill to continue giving it an impression of strength.

The first clue the British had that something was amiss, occurred around ten o'clock the night of August 30th. Sentries in forward observation posts noticed heavy clouds of smoke- or gas, they couldn't be sure which, rolling down the slopes of Kemmel Hill toward their lines. Further observations confirmed that it was indeed smoke after all, and that it came from the Germans burning their supply dumps as they evacuated the hill. Final confirmation of what the Germans were up to, came later that night, when a prisoner – captured near the Hill – spilled everything.

Events now began to unfold quickly. The division was put on alert and the relief of the 60th Brigade was canceled. At nine the next morning, orders were issued for the 119th and 120th regiments to put out patrols across their front, to determine the enemy's location and strength. Each regiment had its objective. The 119th was to reach German lines at the town of Voormezeele, while the 120th was to reach and secure the nearby Lankhaf farm. At 10:30 the first patrols from the 119th began their advance to make contact with the enemy and clinch their objective. The men moved out with bayonets fixed, hearts pounding, every muscle tense as they cautiously moved forward. The experienced Germans were patient.

They waited until the "Old Hickory" boys had covered twenty-five, fifty, seventy-five, and finally, a hundred yards, before they pulled their triggers. Suddenly, the morning air became filled with the terrifying chatter of enemy machine gun fire, and the zip, zip, zip of bullets slicing through the air. Other new sounds were heard too, as bullets found their mark with a sickening thud. Men began to scream and fall.

Somehow, despite the heavy fire, the German lines were reached, resulting in brutal hand to hand combat. The regimental history grimly noted that after the fighting, many of the German dead had bayonet wounds. The attack became too difficult to sustain, and the doughboys were ordered to halt, and wait for artillery support and reinforcements. For the next seven hours or better, the men waited for orders to resume their advance. Meanwhile, reinforcing platoons came up, and British artillery delivered a heavy barrage on German lines. Finally at 7:00 P.M., with darkness approaching and a rain beginning to fall, the 1st and 3rd Battalions of the 119th resumed their advance. Throughout the night, in pitch blackness and a soaking rain the boys pressed the attack. The fighting played out in fits and starts all night and into the next morning, until finally, at 8:30, soaked, hungry, and exhausted the 119th captured its objective. The 120th had successfully secured theirs an hour earlier. On September 3rd, the 30th was finally relieved.

The fight had been intense and bloody. Two officers and thirty-five men from the division were killed, adding their blood to the blood-soaked Flanders soil. An additional 128 men were wounded. German losses amounted to 90-100 killed and 200 wounded. The "Old Hickory" Division captured from the enemy a strip of land one mile square, sixteen prisoners, two machine guns, one grenade launcher, and a small quantity of ammo and supplies. The 119th Regimental history proudly recorded that the 119th was the first American unit to start an advance in Belgium, the first to capture prisoners, and the first to take a village.

Kemmel Hill was now in allied hands. Its capture brought the men a real sense of ease as one doughboy, no doubt expressing what everybody thought, said, "It sure is a blessed relief to move around without feeling the German eyes watching you." Yet, as far as the Ypres Salient was concerned, the offensive changed very little. That situation would not change until the end of September, after the unleashing of the "Grand Offensive" on the Hindenburg Line. But territory had been gained, and perhaps just as important, the division had withstood its first real test of battle. Despite fighting under certain handicaps, i.e. the lack of preparation and reconnaissance (due to the quick unfolding of events), not to mention the appalling battle conditions, it was generally agreed that the 30th had handled itself well. They had entered their first real combat operation, and displayed courage and skill. Yes, there was some fine tuning to do, but they had proven themselves as combat veterans. So much so, that the divisional history crowed that "the 30th was on the map as a fighting unit!" Perhaps more importantly, the division commander, General Lewis, made it clear to the British afterwards that he believed the 30th was now ready and able to take its place in the upcoming "Grand Offensive." The British agreed, and after a brief rest, the "Old Hickory" boys would be sent back to the front once more.

This time to break the Hindenburg Line.

Chapter XIII
The Hindenburg Line

German Army Chief of Staff Field Marshal

Paul von Hindenburg

(Photograph courtesy of National World War I Museum.)

Following the Ypres-Lys Offensive, the 30^{th's} days in Belgium was over. In need of rest and additional training, the division was relieved and ordered to re-locate further south in France. Typically, the army brass was silent about their eventual destination and plans, so rumors began to spread, as they always do. A popular one that made the rounds was that the division would be joining their fellow Americans in the A.E.F., but of course, that was not to be the case. On September 3rd, the day after the orders were issued, the 119th made its way to St. Jan-tor (Belgium) and enjoyed a day and a half of badly needed rest and bathing. On the fifth, the entire division assembled at the town of Proven and boarded trains for France. On the 7th, after a fourteen- hour ride the division arrived in St. Pol, a British rest and training sector. Here, the battalions were assigned to their billets, with the 3rd Battalion located at nearby Moncheaux. For training purposes, the division was assigned to the British 1st Army.

A small town of 30,000 people, St. Pol was located just north of Amiens, where the "Hundred day offensive" had begun earlier in August. St. Pol was far enough behind the front, that for the first time in months, the division was out of German artillery range. As the division history gladly noted, "For the first time in many days the booming of the guns was not audible." The division's stay at St. Pol gave the doughboys a much needed break, and some time for R&R, but it was not forgotten there was still a war on and they had a job to do. For the next three weeks, from the time they reached St. Pol, until they took their place for the Hindenburg assault, the 30th was kept busy, preparing for their date with destiny. I would think that, as each day, and each move, brought them ever closer to the main assault, there would have been a growing sense of reality and dread. After all, they had "seen the elephant", as Civil War veterans used to say about the experience of battle. Any illusions they had would've surely been stripped away at Ypres.

For the first ten days the division worked hard on correcting the mistakes made at Kemmel Hill, and preparing for the upcoming assault on the Hindenburg line. Their orders from A.E.F.

headquarters insisted that their training "...will strongly emphasize the attack-which should be devoted the greater part of all exercises from those for the platoon to the division." Accordingly, the men drilled twice a day and practiced attacking enemy positions, especially machine gun nests. It was also here that the division received training in coordinating infantry attacks with tanks. Private Bivins wrote about it in one of his letters, saying "We are going out to watch a maneuver tomorrow: It includes tanks working in connection with infantry. Imagine it will be worth seeing." Like gas and flamethrowers, the tank was another innovation of the war. It was invented by the British and had been used with some success, most notably at Amiens. It was hoped that this new weapon--impervious to machine gun fire-- could finally break the deadlock of trench warfare. Consequently, several tank units would lead the attack on the Hindenburg line. Interestingly, the 119th historians wrote that the tanks were "...not appreciated at the time" but training with them "proved of inestimable value with the subsequent operations of the regiment."

After their ten day stay at St. Pol, events began to accelerate quickly. On the 17th the division made a six hour train trip to Puchevillere (or the Somme) for additional training with the British III Army. On the 22nd, the division transferred to the British IV Army, who would command the 30th throughout the upcoming campaign. They moved out on the 23rd, and after driving all night in Lorries (or busses as we would say), arrived in the Tinecourt area by 6:00 A.M. the next day. After unloading, the men made a four mile hike to the southern edge of a woods northwest of Tinecourt, and for the first time in weeks, came under enemy artillery fire again.

The 30th was in the Nauroy sector, just west of a French town called Bellicourt. Little did they know at the time what role Bellicourt would play in the upcoming fight. The sector had been occupied by Australian troops of the 1st Australian Division, Australian Corps, and the British IV Army. At ten o'clock on the morning of the 24th, the 1st Division was relieved and the 30th took over. On the afternoon of the same day, the 119th was positioned near the shattered village of Roisel. Here they would remain, making final preparations for the assault. Five days later they would truly be "In the thick of it."

Lying several miles behind the Western Front and stretching over one hundred miles from Flanders in the north to Verdun in the south, ran the dreaded Hindenburg Line. Construction on this massive defensive system began in 1916, following the Battle of the Somme, and the resulting change in German thinking. Believing that a single trench line resulted in too many casualties, Generals Erich Ludendorff and Paul Von Hindenburg conceived of a far more vast and deadly defense. The system consisted of layers of trenches (three or better), each backing the other and linked by communication trenches. Collectively, it extended back as much as 15 kilometers or 9.5 miles. Thick as a jungle, barbed wire spanned the entire length of the trenches as well as between them. Fronting the system were the outpost trenches, or "outpost Line", designed to slow down, weaken, and disorganize an attack. At roughly a half mile to the rear of the outpost line, was the main battle zone, one and a half mile deep! It was heavily fortified with concrete blockhouses, bristling with machine guns. In case any attacker survived this death zone, there was an additional line further back with even more machine gun nests, and artillery ready to cut them down. Not surprisingly, the German high command believed the Hindenburg Line to be impregnable.

Across its length, the Hindenburg Line was subdivided into five zones, or "stellungs" as the Germans called them. Honoring their Nordic roots, each stellung was named after ancient Nordic deities from Richard Wagner's opera "Der Ring des Nibelungen." Working its way from north to south, they were the following: Wotan, Siegfried, Alberich, Brunhilde, and Kriemhilde stellungs. Interestingly, the Germans never referred to the system as the Hindenburg line. That was a British contrivance, obviously referencing General Hindenburg, who played a key role in the development of the system.

By the fall of 1918, the Hindenburg Line was all that stood

between the allied armies and the "Fatherland". Just as significantly, the Antwerp-Metz railroad ran behind the Hindenburg Line along the entire length of the German front. It was Germany's Achilles Heel. That vital rail line was the German's army main supply line and his escape route back to Germany. If the allies could penetrate the line it would bring Germany to her knees. Once taken, the Germans had nothing left to stop an allied advance onto German soil. Quite simply, the Hindenburg Line was Germany's last hope.

Prior to America's involvement, attacking the Hindenburg Line would've been unthinkable. But, by the autumn of 1918, with America's two million man army in France, the allies finally had both the initiative and numbers to get the job done. "Tout le monde a la Batille" General Foch ordered; "Everyone into the battle!"

The plan for Foch's "Grand Offensive," as it was called, was as follows: Between September 26th and 29th, a wave of allied hammer blows aimed at the various Stellungs would be unleashed. Starting in the south between Reims and Verdun, in what became known as the Meuse-Argonne offensive, a French and American army would launch its attack. Further north, with King Leopold of Belgium fittingly leading the assault, a combined Belgian, French, and British army would attack in Flanders. Finally, in the middle of the line, a largely British force would attack the strongest portion of the line. Three British armies (the I, III, and IV, of which the American II corps belonged) and one French army, all under the overall command of General Douglas Haig, would strike at the Siegfried Line, between Cambrai and St. Quentin. Thusly, the line from the Argonne to Ypres would be under tremendous pressure, preventing German units from shifting elsewhere to bolster the line. Eventually the line would have to crack. The question was where?

Even though the II Corps would play a very important part in the breaking of the Hindenburg Line, their accomplishments, which were considerable, are overshadowed by the Meuse-Argonne offensive further south. Here in the United States, if anyone knows anything about that war, it's likely rooted in that campaign, and for good reason. It was the only campaign in the "Grand Offensive" that was fought by an American army under American command. Naturally, when the folks back home read their morning paper, that's what they wanted to know about. Plus, it was the Meuse-Argonne Offensive that gave us some of our most famous exploits and heroes of the war. This is where we get the epic tale of Sgt. York, the Tennessean sharpshooter, whose exploits earned him the Medal of Honor, and made him the subject of a popular Hollywood movie. This is where we also get the tragic story of the "Lost Battalion" who were surrounded, fought desperately, but lived to tell the tale. The Meuse-Argonne Offensive is also where we get future generals like Douglas McArthur, George C. Marshall, and George Patton, gaining valuable experiences that they will put to use in another world war. And finally, this is where Missouri farmer and future President, Harry S. Truman, served as captain of artillery, Battery D. Unfortunately, it's no wonder the story of the 30th Division gets lost in the telling.

As the brave men of the II Corps braced themselves for the upcoming attack on the Hindenburg Line, they could stare out across the open, rolling terrain of the forbidding defenses of the Siegfried line. The landscape the enemy occupied was tailor-made for defensive fighting, with its open spaces, ridges, valleys, and sunken roads. There was little, if any, cover. What fences or hedges there had been, had been removed by the Germans. Only a few trees and the occasional house occupied the landscape. Indeed, what they were looking at was the strongest and most complex portion of the entire Hindenburg system!

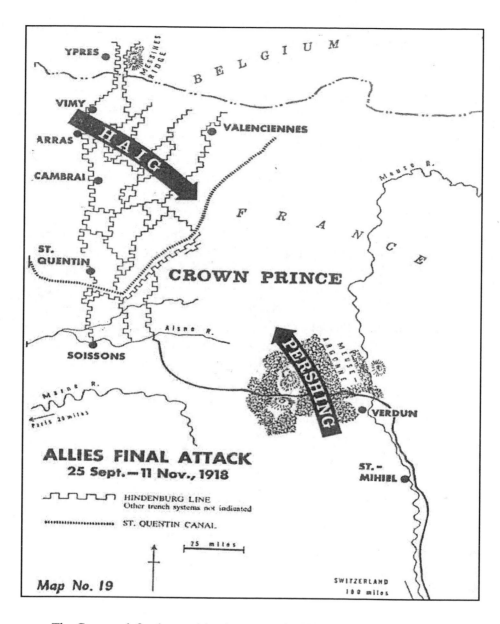

The German defensive position known as the Hindenburg Line, stretched from Flanders to Verdun.

135

If they looked harder, they might've also seen a canal and a tunnel running through the defenses, which the Germans had cleverly integrated into their defensive scheme. As fate would have it, it would be the assigned task of the II Corps to attack this part of the line, the strongest section, of the strongest position in *the entire Hindenburg Line*.

The waterway that ran through the Siegfried line was the St. Quentin canal. It flowed lazily through the countryside in a southerly direction from Cambrai to St. Quentin. Just west of the village of LeCatelet, and north of Bellicourt, the canal entered a tunnel and would not emerge again until three miles later at Riqueval. Its origins dated back to 1769, but it wasn't until 1809, during the Napoleonic era, that construction was finally completed. Made of concrete, this engineering feat was massive. Inside, the tunnel reached a height of twenty yards, with a ten yard span at the top, and a width of eighteen yards at water level. The water flowing through had a depth of five to six feet, and once you exited the tunnel, the banks flanking the canal reached a height of seventy -five to one hundred feet. For over a century, the locals had used the canal to leisurely float people and goods throughout the region. But now it had a more sinister purpose, serving as the primary feature in the Siegfried line.

The Germans used the tunnel to house a division of soldiers and to provide a system of smaller tunnels with hidden entrances and exits, to link various positions in the line. Like a prairie dog village, troops could move quickly, safely, and undetected to emerge above ground, and reinforce any threatened position in the line. There were even concrete tunnels, connecting the tunnel with the heavily fortified town of Bellicourt in the rear. Should an attacking force overrun the tunnel, German troops could easily rise up from behind and attack in the rear, causing great confusion and harm. Being so far underground, the tunnel also had the added advantage of providing absolute safety against shelling. Numerous canal barges floated throughout the tunnel, providing living quarters for the troops. To sustain this enormous subterranean force, large store rooms, offices, dressing stations, and kitchens were built into the tunnel walls. And so there was to some degree comfort: the tunnel was ventilated, heated, and wired for electric light.

Above ground, a massive trench system overlapped the St. Quentin canal and tunnel. Immediately west of the tunnel, spanning a zone of 1000 yards (over three football fields) was the main line of defense. Commanding all approaches, and spaced about 50 - 60 yards apart, were concrete pill boxes, bristling with machine guns. A mile further west of the main line was the outpost zone. Fortified just as heavily, the two lines were linked by numerous communication trenches. East of the main line, and running behind the canal and through the town of Nauroy, was yet another line called the LeCatelet-Nauroy, (or Hindenburg Reserve) line. Finally, protecting it all, were miles of barbed wire, fifty to one hundred fifty yards deep.

The defenses did indeed appear to be impregnable, and the men of the 30th could be forgiven if they thought they were being sent on a suicide mission. However, in an extraordinary piece of luck, on August 8th, weeks before the attack, the British captured a copy of the German defense plan. It described in great detail the enemy defenses from the Oise River further south, to Bellicourt. It revealed the positions of every battery, observation posts, machine gun emplacements, infantry and artillery HQ, and much more. Oddly, neither the division, nor regimental histories, or any of my other sources say what impact, if any, this find had. But it must have. Such valuable information would've made it possible for British artillery to take out many of these key positions before sending in the boys, thereby reducing the risks. It's beyond imaging that the British wouldn't have used this, and it must've of made some difference in the end.

The assault on this middle portion of the Hindenburg Line was actually four separate battles over an eleven- day period, which can be quite confusing, as each battle has its own name, and is often used interchangeably. But the basic idea was this. At the northern extreme of the sector, from September 27th to October 1st, the British opened the offensive with the Battle of Canal Du Nord. Moving southward, the British IV army, with its American II Corps and Australian 5th Division, and French 1st Armies, would fight the Battle of St. Quentin from September 29th to October 2nd. Even further south, another British army would fight the Battle of Beaurevoir on October 3rd to the 6th. And finally, on October 8th-9th, the British will fight the Battle of Cambrai. Confusing the matter even more, the Battle for the Hindenburg Line is often called the Battle of Cambrai-St. Quentin. Some sources will even refer to it at the Battle of Bellicourt, after the town that sat in the middle of the German defenses. In fact, Grandpa's discharge papers never mention the Hindenburg Line, but lists Bellicourt instead. In any case, regardless of what it was called, these multiple attacks will be massive, involving thousands of men in fifty two allied divisions, up against fifty- seven German divisions. The resulting battle would be desperate, savage, bloody, and in the end, decisive. For those who fought and survived that awful day, what they saw and did would sear itself into their souls forever.

For Grandpa, it was a day he would never forget.

Chapter XIV

In The Thick Of It!

They fought like seasoned veterans, like warriors they fell;
They stormed the battlements of death;
they charged the gates of hell;

And laid the haughty legionnaires of Hindenburg supine;
And the world sang "Yankee Doodle," when the Yankees
broke the line.

While it was the British IV Army who was in charge of operations in front of the Siegfried line, it was Australian Lt. General John Monash who was given the job of planning the attack. Believing that an attack over the canal itself would be too costly, he decided to focus the assault on the tunnel, which formed a "bridge" over the canal, and provided access to Bellicourt and the reserve trenches. The operation would be very complex, and it required experienced troops like his own Australian Corps, but almost continuous combat since August had left it exhausted. That left him with the relatively fresh and experienced Australian 3rd and 5th Divisions, and the relatively inexperienced, American II Corps. While Ypres and Kemmel Hill had given the 30th some combat experience, they had never participated in an operation as large or complicated as this one would be. Tragically, the lack of experience would take a terrible toll in the ensuing battle, and Monash would later be roundly criticized for his decisions; Nonetheless, the attack would proceed as he planned it.

The assault on the Hindenburg Line would unfold in two phases. The first phase consisted of attacking and taking the outpost zone, which would give the division what was called a "good line of departure". This meant they would be in a better position, that is to say, closer to the enemy with less ground to cover, when the time came for the main assault. The second phase would be the main attack itself on the line. Monash's plan called for the numerically superior 27th and 30th Divisions to spearhead the attack, break the line, and capture the reserve Hindenburg line. Then, while they paused to re-group their forces, the fresh Australian divisions would pass through the breach and continue the drive, keeping the Germans on their heels. Keenly aware of the dangers the hidden tunnels and dugouts presented to advancing troops, Monash stressed in his orders, that the regiments should attack with two battalions, and use a third to follow behind and "mop up." In other words, root out, capture and disarm, or kill any German found threatening the rear of the attack. He knew from hard experience, that in the confusion of battle, his troops could easily overrun and bypass hidden dugouts only to have the enemy surface and shoot his boys in the back. In fact, as the battle progressed, this would be a deadly problem for both divisions.

The battle plan called for the two American divisions to

occupy a four mile front, with each division assigned a zone of operations of roughly 2-2.5 miles each. The 27th would be positioned on the left flank of the 30th. Following a massive artillery barrage, each division would have to cross approximately a thousand yards (a little over nine football fields), under heavy enemy fire and capture their objectives. For the 27th it would be the town of Bony, while the 30th would target Bellicourt. The date for the main attack was set for dawn, Sunday, September 29th.

On September 24th and 25th, the two American divisions moved into their respective zones, and took their places in the line. Despite their common goals, each division was confronted with a different set of circumstances that would ultimately shape the battle each would fight. As stated before, the first phase of the battle would be the capture of the outpost zone and the securing of a good line of departure. In this regard, the 30th was very fortunate. Days before, the British had successfully taken a large portion of the outpost zone that fronted the 30th. On the evening of the 26th the division advanced an additional 300 yards and took control of Quary Woods and a nearby trench. With this success, the 30th had its favorable line of departure. For the poor 27th however, it would be an entirely different story.

Despite several attacks, the British failed in taking the outpost zone facing the 27th. Following these failures, the 27th then was ordered to attack on Friday the 27th, and seize the strong points of Quennemont and Guillemont Farms, and a nearby knoll. To reach them, the division would have to cross a mile and a half of open ground. At 5:30 AM, the attack began.

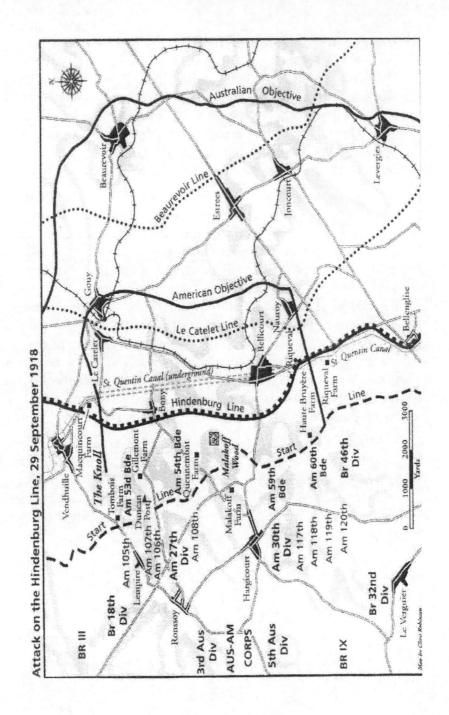

Attack on the Hindenburg Line, 29 September 1918

Australian Objective

Beaurevoir

Levergies

Beaurevoir Line

Estrees

Joncourt

Gouy

American Objective

Bellenglise

Le Catelet Line

Bellicourt

Nauroy

Riqueval

St. Quentin Canal

Le Catelet

St. Quentin Canal (underground)

Bony

Hindenburg Line

Haute Bruyère Farm

Riqueval Farm

Line

Macquincourt Farm

The Knoll

Gillemont Farm

Am 54th Bde

Malakoff Wood

Start

Am 60th Bde

Br 46th Div

Vendhuille

Tombois Farm

Am 53d Bde

Quennemont Farm

3000

Duncan

Am 107th Post

Line

Am 59th Bde

2000

Start

Lempire

Am 105th

Am 106th

Am 27th Div

Am 108th

Malakoff Farm

Am 30th Div

Am 117th

Am 118th

Am 119th

1000

Yards

Br 18th Div

Hargicourt

Am 120th

0

Ronssoy

3rd Aus Div

AUS-AM CORPS

5th Aus Div

Br IX

Br 32nd Div

Le Verguier

BR III

Map by Clive Robinson

Tanks rolling on the way to participate in the attack on the Hindenburg Line at Bellincourt.

The entire area was "covered by wide belts of strong German barb wire; even communications trenches being heavily wired."

The Germans were well entrenched as shown by this machine gun nest taken out that "covered the entrance to the St. Quentin Canal Tunnel at an angle of about 60 yards."

The German trenches ran for miles; strongly reinforced with huge concrete blocks. Shown also are the wooden fire steps.

The St. Quentin Canal and entrance to the tunnel at Riqueval, near Bellicourt, France. October 18, 1918

The village of Bellicourt along the St. Quentin Canal. Note troops on the roads entering the town. Tunnel and canal in the bottom center of the photograph.

Supported by tanks and artillery fire, the brave New Yorkers advanced under extremely heavy enemy fire. They were able to gain footholds at the respective farms and the knoll, but fierce counterattacks forced many of the attackers to fall back. By the end of the day, the attack had failed, and while most of the division had withdrawn, there were numerous pockets of doughboys left behind, tenuously holding their ground. The fighting had been desperate and causalities had been in the extreme. Two men of the 27th, 1st Lt. William B. Turner and Sgt. Reider Waller, would receive the Medal of Honor for their actions that day.

The failure to take the outpost zone would have dire consequences for the 27th, when the main attack came on Sunday. That, and the fact that so many troops were stranded on the battle field, would shape how the main attack would unfold. These circumstances confronting the high command left them with a terrible decision to make. Should they launch the main attack with close- in artillery support, and risk killing their own men left behind from the previous attack? Or, should they send in their men without any close in artillery protection, and expose them to vicious enemy fire? It was a hell of a decision to make, but the commanders knew they could not risk shelling their own men. When the time came, the division would go in without close-in artillery support.

Meanwhile, final preparations were being made for the main assault. On Y/Z night, the 28th in other words, under the cover of darkness, a detachment of engineers slipped out of the trenches forty yards into "no man's land", and laid in place a length of white tape in front of their lines. Running parallel to their trenches, it would serve as a departure line for the troops to line up on prior to the attack. Evidently, it also served to assist with the upcoming barrage. In a 1976 interview with the *Vandalia Leader,* Grandpa recalled the engineers laying down the "6 inch" tape for miles. The men, he said, had been ordered to stay behind the tape until it was time for the assault. And, in what must have been a sobering piece of news, they were also told the big guns in the rear had elevated their barrels so the shells would fall just beyond the tape at two hundred yards. Indeed, the attack would begin with what was called a "rolling barrage" (also known as a creeping barrage), providing close- in artillery support.

An offensive technique that had been developed earlier in the war, rolling barrages had been used with mixed results. Timing was critical for it to be effective, and that's where it sometimes failed. The basic idea was to lay down a curtain of steel ahead of the attacking infantry. The barrage would advance, or "roll" forward at specified intervals, with the infantry attacking from behind at a "safe" distance, thereby offering a protective shield for the attackers. Good idea on paper, but tricky to execute. For it to work, troops had to "lean" into the barrage, that is to say, follow it closely, say within 100 yards, to prevent the enemy time to recover and fight back when the barrage passed them over. If they didn't keep pace, the enemy could catch the attack in the open and destroy it. Complicating matters further was "friendly fire", or shells falling short and blasting your own men. The French believed that if they were doing it right, they should suffer up to 10 percent of their casualties from their own artillery! Similarly, the British were also willing to accept such losses. Oh, what a lovely war!

In their orders for the attack, tanks and infantry were to follow the rolling barrage at a safe seventy yards. Realizing that once the attack began, anything could happen, as battle plans rarely, if ever, go according to plan, their orders also stipulated that the "Action of tanks accompanying supporting troops will be dictated by the situation", as indeed it would be. While rolling barrages were difficult to pull off, at least the 30th would have close in artillery support, something, you will recall, the 27th would tragically lack.

Taking heed of General Monash's warnings, battalion commanders were instructed where they would place their troops on the tape. Grandpa's regiment, the 119th, would have its 1st and 2nd Battalion lined up to lead the attack on their immediate front. Following the attack to mop up overlooked German strong points, as Monash required, would be Grandpa and his comrades of the 3rd

Battalion. Supporting the 119th on their right flank, would be the 120th Regiment, whose battalions were similarly placed. The commander of each battalion assigned mopping up duties were given further instructions in Field Order #28. All men were to wear a "distinctive mark" to identify them (unfortunately it does not elaborate on what the distinctive mark should be). Once the tunnel was reached, they were to cover each entrance and search for unknown entrances and exits, not returning until their crucial work was complete. To assist them in their dangerous work, the order also stipulated that a full supply of smoke bombs and grenades be issued to the men. Meanwhile, all of the men throughout the division were issued 220 rounds of ammunition, and two grenades each. While all of these other preparations were taking place, huge quantities of ammo, food, and other supplies had been steadily moving up to support the attack. Everything was in readiness. All that was left to do now was wait for the Sunday dawn.

Since the days of Alexander, armies have gone through a pre-battle ritual, designed to boost their morale and whip up their fighting spirit. Hot food, and a "pep talk", typically preceded a fight, as commanders tried to inspire their men and calm their nerves. The night of the 28th, for example, the men were served a hot meal with fresh meat. Frequently, church services were held, as soldiers tried to make peace with their god before meeting an uncertain fate. My mother once told me that on one occasion, Grandpa served as an altar boy for a front line service. Was it before this battle, I wonder? After meeting the physical and spiritual needs of the men, officers would try to prepare them psychologically for combat with a speech. The men would dutifully listen, and if suitably impressed, give a cheer. Individual officers had their own style. Some might be bombastic and profane, while others might be more soft-spoken. In a typical speech the officers would remind their men of their duty to God, country, family, and each other (The British would throw in the king for good measure). Final instructions might be given, such as keeping their heads down, keep moving, and not to assist the wounded. And some would try to inspire their men with some tough talk, as did Colonel Metts of the 119th. "Break that line", he barked, *or not a one of us comes back!*" It's not recorded, unfortunately, if the men cheered their commander's, spartanesque order, or not. In any case, all that could be done, had been done. The only thing left to do now, was break that line.

On Saturday, September 28th, shortly before midnight, the two divisions made their final movements for battle. With planes flying overhead to conceal the sound of their movement, British Mark V tanks, rumbling and clanking, lurched their way forward to the tape. Then, at 4:30 AM, quickly and silently, thousands of anxious doughboys clambered out of their trenches, and moved single file through the openings in their wire, to also take their places along the tape. They were now in "no-man's" land, with the enemy directly in front of them. It must have been a moment full of anticipation, and suspense--surreal even. All they had trained for, all of the immense preparation that preceded this, had finally come down to this moment. The magnitude of what they were about to do could not have been lost on any man. And, even if it was, they would have had nearly an hour and a half to lie there in the gloomy darkness, and think about it.

It must've been terrible to lie there and wait. The air would have been heavy with suspense and dread, as each tick of the clock brought them ever closer to their fates. They say the anticipation of a fight is worse than the fight itself. Every man reacts differently to such pre-battle stress. Some try to joke or indulge in nervous chatter, while others become deeply silent. Some, experiencing a premonition of their death, would plead with a buddy to deliver a message to a loved one back home. Certainly there would've been plenty of thoughts of home, and loved ones left behind. Many would wonder if they would ever see them again. There would have been little for them to do to help them release their nervous energy. Smoking was banned, as lit cigarettes could've been seen by the enemy. Maybe they chewed, as Grandpa might have. Of course, many would have prayed. Like they say, there's no atheists in foxholes. I'm sure Grandpa did. I wonder, being the good Catholic that he was, did he have a rosary to pray with? Surely, he thought of his family, who at that hour would've been sleeping safely in their beds, it being about 9:30 P.M., Oconee time. Sgt. Melville of the 27th Division, no doubt spoke for everyone, when he described his feelings that night, saying, "We had to lie there all night and worry. It is impossible to describe the feelings a man has with that in front of him. I always said I knew how a man felt who was condemned to die. *For we all* thought it was our last night...."

As the fateful hour drew closer, the men would've experienced sweating, rapidly beating hearts, shallow breathing, and in some cases-loose bowels. Grandpa once told me he witnessed a man "dirty his pants". The idea that a man could be so scared, he would literally shit his pants, had never occurred to me before Grandpa shared that little nugget. It was yet another illusion of war I was disabused of. Being in the war business a long time, the British were fully aware of the stress the men felt, and had their own unique way of helping them cope. On the eve of battle, each man of the 27th was given a half tumbler of rum to help steady their nerves. I assume the 30th received the same consideration.

To men like Sgt. Melville, who felt like they were condemned to die, dawn must have come all too soon. By 5:45 AM, a dense, autumn fog had settled over "no-man's land", giving it a more foreboding appearance. As the silver streaks of dawn began to appear on the eastern horizon, thousands of doughboys laid still on the cold, damp ground and waited. Officers nervously checked their watches one more time, bracing themselves for the inevitable. Then, at 5:50 AM-zero hour-a red signal flare shot up in the sky. For a brief moment time stood still, as thousands held their breath and waited. Suddenly, the world exploded, as the guns of fourteen artillery brigades spoke as one, sending their shells screaming through the morning air. The shells screamed over the prone men, landing with a shocking violence two hundred yards away. The 119th regimental history described it "As the most terrific barrage ever laid down on the Western Front."

A few minutes later, German artillery responded in kind, its shells landing directly behind the men, hitting their empty front line trenches-yet another reason for the tape! Caught in a terrifying crossfire, the ground, Grandpa said, began to *"boil like a volcano!"* Huge geysers of earth blew skyward, as each shell exploded, blasting out craters big enough to drop a house into. Adding its own voice to the awful din, were planes flying overhead dropping bombs on the enemy below. The noise was terrible and overwhelming. Colonel Metts described it as "a hell of torturing sound." To the brave men caught in the middle of the shelling, it was terrifying. All they could do was hug the shaking ground, and try to make themselves invisible. Time stood still, as each concussive wave swept over them with gut wrenching ferocity. To experience a bombardment, is to experience a profound sense of helplessness. All a man can do is grit his teeth, and pray that the next shell doesn't have his name on it, and blow him to atoms. For one terrified doughboy, the shelling was so overwhelming, that he cried out into the storm for his mother. Desperate and helpless, Grandpa's voice was hopelessly swallowed up by the pitiless roar. Yet, thousands of miles away, Mary Rakers heard something in her sleep. Deeply troubled, she rose out of bed, and summoned her family together.

Meanwhile, on the left flank of the 30th, the men of the 27th Division, spaced five yards apart and with bayonets fixed, began their advance. Following in the wake of their tanks, they charged into the outpost zone. British artillery fired salvos at German positions *behind* the knoll and Quennemont and Guillemont farms, but could not provide a rolling barrage to protect the attack. The division was terribly exposed. To have any artillery protection at all, it had to cover 1,200 yards in four minutes, before the barrage lifted and crept forward. Blocking their way of course were countless machine gun nests. It was a recipe for slaughter. By the time the division reached the knoll, the division's entire front was swept with withering machine gun and artillery fire. One survivor described the fire, as "thicker than flies in the summer." The tanks were of little help, as anti-tank guns and mines quickly knocked them out, one by one, with shocking ease. The fight quickly became, as the authors of *American Armies and Battlefields in*

154

Europe wrote, "One vast maelstrom of violence."

Despite the terrible pounding the 27th was taking, it continued to press the attack with tremendous heroism. After all of the members of his squad had been killed, Pvt. Frank Gaffney rushed an enemy machine gun nest, killed the entire crew, captured the gun, and blasted several dugouts with grenades before killing four more of the enemy with his pistol. He held his position until reinforcements arrived, whereupon they captured eighty of the enemy.

When his unit was pinned down by German machine gun fire, Pvt. Michael Valente volunteered to go forward. Braving intense machine gun fire, Valente and Pvt. Joseph Mastine rushed a machine gun nest and silenced the gun. Nearby, another machine gun nest was pouring deadly fire into the desperate doughboys. Once again, Valente and his comrade charged the gun, and destroyed it, before jumping into the enemy trench and killing two more, and capturing sixteen Germans. Luckily for the Germans, he was eventually wounded and removed from the field. For their heroic actions Gaffney and Valente both received the Medal of Honor, while Mastine would be awarded the Distinguished Service Cross. As Gaffney's and Valente's heroism attests, the fighting at the knoll and Guillemont Farm was desperate and bloody. By day's end, the 107th Regiment alone, of which both men belonged, had 337 men killed and 658 wounded, almost a third of its strength. This gave the 107th the dubious distinction of being the only American regiment during the war to suffer such high losses in a single day.

Meanwhile the "old Hickory" boys were engaged in a bloodbath of their own.

After what must have seemed like an interminable time span of only four minutes, the barrage lifted, and began to roll forward as planned. The tanks, looking like giant steel slugs, lurched forward into the fray, their treads chewing into the wire, making paths for the men. The officers, blowing whistles and screaming to be heard, ordered their men forward. Thousands of doughboys, their Enfields clutched in their hands and their hearts in their throats, charged ahead, trance- like, struggling to stay within seventy yards of the shelling. As the tanks and men worked their way forward, they were swallowed up by the thick morning fog. Between the fog and the shelling (which included a smoke barrage), the battlefield became nearly invisible. The divisional history claimed that the men could only see five yards in any direction. It was so bad, Grandpa told the *Vandalia Leader,* and later, me, that "It was noon before the smoke cleared enough so we could see the sun." The divisional history dramatically described the scene: "Men seemed like wraiths, spectral shapes that formed before the eyes, only to slip eerily from sight into the thickening gloom." The fog did offer the advantage of making the men harder to see by the enemy. Nonetheless, it also resulted in the overlooking of many enemy strong points, a mistake that would have deadly consequences.

All was noise and chaos. The divisional history described the attack as a "direful symphony of battle" with the "scream of bursting shrapnel, the whistle of bullets, the splintering explosions of grenades, the staccato bark of countless machine guns " and the "reverberating boom of heavy siege guns" filling the air. The attack quickly broke down as fog, smoke, shell craters and heavy enemy fire all conspired to make any cohesive forward movement impossible. Colonel Metts of the 119th later wrote that it would never be known how his brave boys fought their way through the wire, shell holes, and trenches. The attack splintered into countless small engagements as officers, NCO's and enlisted men alike, exhibited great initiative and courage, and led their comrades against the next obstacle. Each conquest was paid for in blood, as the men crawled, cussed, screamed, shot, blasted, and bayoneted their way through countless machine gun nests, bunkers, and trenches. Their forward progress, Metts starkly observed, left "bits of clothing and flesh" in the wires.

It was a day when extraordinary courage was ordinary. One hundred and twenty Distinguished Service Crosses, and two Medal of Honors will attest to that. Fifty three, or 44 percent of the

DSC's recipients that day, came from the 119th Regiment. Grandpa's Company K, contributed four to that total. As I read over the *sixty* pages of citations in the divisional history, I was struck by how similar the stories were. Again and again, men risked their lives attacking machine gun nests, rescuing a wounded buddy, or serving as a runner, delivering messages. Phrases such as "Braved enemy fire"; "Defended his post single handedly"; "Continued to fight despite his wounds"; "Repeatedly carried messages"; "Refused evacuation", appear consistently throughout the citations. Here are a few of their stories.

Enjoying the relative safety of the division's forward observation post. Major Walter Hartigan of the 118th Regiment watched the attack unfold. He became increasingly disturbed as he saw his men losing their direction in the heavy fog. Without hesitation he volunteered to leave is post and re-organize his men. With explosions blasting all around and bullets zipping past him, he successfully organized several hundred stragglers of the 60th Brigade, as well as two companies of the 117th regiment. After securing two tanks to assist them, he led these units back into the battle.

Forty three citations involved a man taking out a machine gun nest. Sgt. Milo Lemert of the 119th, located the gun that had been creating heavy casualties, and holding up his company's left flank. Braving enemy fire, he rushed the nest single-handedly and killed the crew with grenades. As he continued along the enemy trench, he found another nest and destroyed it as well. Immediately from his left, another machine gun fired at him. Once again Lemert destroyed it with grenades. Sometime later, with the aid of another Sgt., he attacked a fourth machine gun nest. As he reached the parapet of the emplacement, his luck ran out, and he was killed.

Sgt. Joseph Adikinson, also to the 119th, saw his platoon pinned down by murderous machine gun fire. Alone, he charged across fifty yards of open ground, kicked the gun from the parapet into the trench, and at the point of a bayonet, captured the three man crew. His platoon continued its advance. For these actions,

157

both men were awarded the Medal of Honor.

Many of the recipients showed a different kind of courage that day, risking their lives coming to the aid of the wounded. Pvt. Andrew Varner of the 119th, for example. When intense enemy shelling caused two stretcher bearers to abandon a wounded comrade (not all were brave that day), Pvt. Varner knew what he had to do. Forcing two German prisoners to go with him, he dashed across seventy- five yards of flying shrapnel, and rescued his comrade. Captain George Batson of the 118th Regiment also ran across three hundred yards under heavy fire, recovered a wounded man, and brought him back to safety. And stretcher bearer Pvt. John Crofts of the 120th Regiment was so badly wounded in his right arm, that he could not continue his duties. After receiving treatment he continued, despite heavy shelling, to aid the walking wounded.

On the WWI battlefield, runners, or couriers played an important part in delivering messages. It was an extremely dangerous job, and few survived it. Ten men for the 30th received the Distinguished Service Cross as runners that day, two from Grandpa's Company K. When Co. K's H.Q. realized that a portion of the company was in danger of being hit with a German counterattack, a runner was sent to tell them to fall back. He was immediately shot down. Seeing this Cpl. Seth Perry volunteered for the dangerous mission. While crossing an open field under heavy fire, he too was killed. Whereupon, Sgt. George Miller volunteered to go next and make the attempt. As he crossed the same open field, he was also shot down. It's not recorded if the message ever got through.

At 7:30 A.M., after nearly two hours of desperate combat, 30th Division HQ's received a field message informing them the 119th Regiment had broken the line! Pressing on, they captured the southern mouth of the tunnel, and finally reached their objective of Bellicourt. After a sharp fight and mopping up, the town was declared secure by 11:45 A.M. Meanwhile, on their right, the 120th Regiment successfully crossed the canal, pushed eastward, and by

11:00 A.M. captured the town of Nauroy, before hard fighting forced it to stop its advance.

Compared to the struggle of the 27th Division, the fighting had been relatively easy for the 30th. Thanks to the Fog, rolling barrage, and the tanks, their advance had happened quickly. Too quickly as it turned out, because in their haste, many enemy strong points had gone overlooked. Just as Monash had feared, warned against, and tried to prepare for, the Germans used their tunnels to surface behind the division, and re-man overrun machine gun posts. They immediately attacked. Reserve units, wire details, runners, and others following the main assaulting waves, were hit hard. With the enemy in their front and rear, the entire division experienced great confusion throughout their zone of action. Countless isolated battles unfolded, as doughboys and tanks tried to coordinate attacks, and take out the deadly nests. Eventually, after much hard fighting, all the Germans found in the rear were either killed or captured.

The quick advance of the 30th presented another problem as well. When the division had advanced far beyond the tunnel, it was realized that the 27th on their left, had not been able to keep up. This created a gap of roughly 1,500 yards, between the 27th Division and the 119th Regiment. Of course, the Germans saw this immediately, and tried to exploit the breach by throwing in reinforcements, in an attempt to get behind the division. Reserve units of the 119th and 118th were hastily thrown in to try and plug the gap. The resulting fight was severe and bloody, with heavy losses. However, "We kept the 'Boche' from working behind us" Colonel Metts proudly wrote, "and held our ground!"

At noon, the Aussies came up to help the 27th Division, and with the two forces attacking together, they were finally able to reach their objective. Pressing the attack, they eventually linked up with the "Old Hickory" boys, and at 3:00 PM, the Australian 5th Division passed through as planned, and continued the advance. With the St. Quentin Canal firmly in allied possession, overall command passed to the Australians, relieving the American II

159

Corps and giving them a much needed rest. As the exhausted Doughboys settled in for the night, a heavy, cold rain began to fall.

It had been a terrible day. The regimental historians wrote that the battlefield "Presented a miserable appearance." One "Old Hickory" soldier wrote in his diary;

"Scores of dead Americans and Australians, and Germans can be seen lying about the field, some covered with raincoats and overcoats, while others lie just as they fell. Walking wounded are going back in twos and threes, while those unable to walk are being carried off the field as rapidly as possible under the circumstances. Men with arms shot off, with slight shrapnel wounds in the face and slightly wounded in the body are being helped to the rear by German prisoners and by other men similarly wounded. Dead horses are lying here and there, but I fail to notice any wounded ones, for they are killed by their drivers as soon as they get hit so they can't travel."

Nothing was left standing. Not a telephone pole, not a tree, not a building. Bellicourt was in ruins. The shell holes were so numerous, the regimental history claimed, that no one could walk three paces without falling into one. It was as if a tsunami had swept over the land, leaving nothing in its wake. The butcher's bill was high that day. Grandpa's 119th Regiment lost 146 men killed, with 691 wounded*. His Company K lost thirteen men. The division as a whole lost approximately 357 men, with 2,575 wounded. Two days of fighting cost the 27th Division, 674 men.

Yet, they had done what the Germans swore they could never do: they had broken the vaunted Hindenburg Line at its strongest point! Not only that, but the division had also advanced 3,000 yards, captured 47 officers and 1,432 men, and seized vast quantities of weapons, ammo , and other materials. Pershing's faith had paid off, although at a terrible price. There was still a lot of hard fighting up ahead--another forty- three days before the armistice – but finally the light could be seen at the end of the tunnel. At 10:00, the morning of the attack, while the battle was still raging, Generals Hindenburg and Ludendorff met with the

German foreign minister and demanded an armistice before the German army faced catastrophe. No doubt they shared the sentiment of the captured German officer, who, when finally convinced that the line had indeed been broken, cried out in despair, *"All is lost-there is nothing between you and the Rhine!"*

It was over, and they knew it.

*There is a discrepancy between the divisional and regimental histories regarding losses for the 119th regiment, with the divisional source showing fewer losses. I decided to go with the figures the Regimental history gave, thinking that since it was only concerned with the regiment, and not the division a whole, it would have more accurate figures. I relied on the divisional history for divisional losses.

Many years later, the summer of 1985 I believe, I had gone to Ramsey to visit my grandparents. School had let out for the summer, and with my teaching duties over for a few months, I liked to spend time with Grandpa and Grandma and enjoy small town life for a while. One day grandma experienced chest pains, so Grandpa and I drove her to the hospital in nearby Pana. She was admitted, and after a brief stay Grandpa and I headed back home. As we were riding along he suddenly spoke. Oddly, what he was about to tell me came unsolicited, as we were not talking about the war. Perhaps the anxiety Grandpa felt over Grandma prompted him to open up. I don't know. Nonetheless, he clearly was experiencing strong emotions, and I believe it triggered a powerful memory he decided to reveal to me.

He began by recalling the opening barrage that terrible September dawn. Then, unbelievably, my normally quiet and reserved Grandfather, began to cry. Shocked, I listened as he managed to choke out how he called out for his mother that day; *"Oh mother, mother!"* he sobbed. Transfixed, I listened as he continued. Upon his return to Oconee, his mother told him, that, one night as she lay sleeping, she heard him cry out to her. Frightened, and knowing something was wrong, she awoke her sleeping family, and gathered them in the kitchen. There, they got down on their knees, and fervently prayed for his safe return. His homecoming was proof to her that God had heard a mother's prayer that night.

That was it. Grandpa didn't say anymore. He didn't have to, as he clearly believed that his mother heard him, and that her prayers saved his life that awful day. I was stunned. Not only at the story itself, but at the depth of emotion he revealed to me. As we drove home in silence, I realized how everything had changed for me. Grandpa's war was no longer quaint stories about dodging drill, or going AWOL with a buddy. For the first time, I saw just how terrible that war really was, and how deeply it affected him. Somewhere from deep inside his soul, a sixty- six year old nightmare had broken through his stoicism, and caused him to break down in front of his grandson. The war changed him. How could it not? He saw his buddies butchered by the score, and he experienced a fear so gut -wrenching, that it could, well, make a man "dirty" his pants. Yet, I think there was something more. Loss of faith can be another casualty of war. I don't know what condition Grandpa's faith was in that bloody September day, but I do believe that what he experienced, and his mother's faith, ultimately deepened *his* faith in God. And that, I believe, had a lot to do with his tears that unforgettable summer day.

Chapter XV

Armistice

Newspapers back home proudly boasts the martial achievements of
"Old Hickory."

Despite the breaking of the Hindenburg Line the war would grind on, as they often do, for another forty- three days. Throughout October and November the British would continue their advance, keeping the pressure on the retreating Germans. For Grandpa and the rest, it would be over a month of being rotated in and out of the line as the high command shuffled them around. For the II Corps, it was a period of hard marching, mud, blood, and mounting casualties. They would have been seasoned veterans by now: tougher, weary, calloused, but no less fearful than before, maybe even more. With the German army on the run they must have sensed the end was near, and nobody wants to be the last casualty, especially in the "war to end all wars."

What did Grandpa experience during this period? It's hard to say. We can assume the obvious: that he was cold, wet, hungry, homesick, and scared, but other than that the record is once again, frustratingly thin. His 1976 interview with the *Vandalia leader* helps a little. He spoke of battling through a small village with explosions all around and buildings collapsing. He had taken cover behind a bombed out church and was firing his rifle, when he saw a one pounder gun unit move in. As he stared at the crew, he was able to make out a familiar form. Lo and behold! It was Orville! The two Oconee boys recognized each other instantly. They may have waved, but it's unlikely they had time to catch up.

On another occasion during the advance, Grandpa saw British cavalry come riding through. Imagine that! In an age of machine guns and tanks, horse cavalry was still being used. In any case, seeing those magnificent, thundering horses with their skilled riders, made a vivid impression on him. Forty two years after the war, he still recalled with admiration the "horsemen with their fine steeds, armed with a saber, rifle and pistol, and each animal carrying a bundle of hay behind the saddle." It must have been a glorious sight. However, the next day that romantic image was jarringly replaced with a far crueler one as he began to see dead cavalrymen and horses. Some of the poor animals were missing chunks of flesh from their hindquarters, mute testimony that they had provided a meal for some hungry, and less sentimental soldier.

He related another story to the paper, one which he told me several times. He had been assigned sentry duty in the forward area so he took up residence in a shell hole. Later that night when his relief came, he climbed out of his hole and deliberately left his rifle and bayonet. When I asked why he would do such a thing he said he could find guns anywhere. Not a very satisfying answer, but I figured he must have been awful tired and didn't want to carry that damn thing anymore than he had to. Writing about this story, and the others, made me see a side of Grandpa I hadn't noticed before. There was the bit of the rebel in Grandpa. Avoiding registration, and later drill, eating the tomato, going AWOL, and leaving his weapon behind all reveal a pattern of rebellion. I can't help but wonder if this was typical behavior of his as a young man, or if the army and the war brought it out in him.

There were other stories he'd tell me that never made it into the newspaper; like the close calls he experienced. One time a German bullet creased the back of his head, shaving the hair off. Another time shrapnel tore through his pack. He described how the weeds would pop up as machine gun bullets cut them down like wheat before a scythe. He recalled seeing aerial dogfights and observation balloons shot flaming out of the sky. He told of giving a wounded buddy water from his canteen. And one story I'll always remember, because he told it with such sad disbelief, was seeing stretcher bearers, needing to retrieve more wounded, callously dump a dead comrade by the side of the road. Those days between Bellicourt and the Armistice created a mosaic of horror which would stay with Grandpa for the rest of his life.

On Monday, September 30th, the day after Bellicourt, the Australian forces launched a new attack on the reeling Germans. Meanwhile, the exhausted II corps was ordered back from the front so their officers could reorganize their badly scattered commands. The next day, October 1st, the 30th Division received orders to fall back even further to the LeMesnil and Herbecourt areas for a much needed rest. Orville wrote a little about these rest periods behind the front. He noted that, typically, they were located in a small village out of range of the big guns. They would often stay in the villagers homes, which usually were made of stone. Quite often, the homes were attached to the barn, and in what must have been a culture shock, he observed that the families would live on the second floor, while the livestock occupied the first. Despite his inability to speak French, he could tell the locals were glad they were there. On several occasions he and Grandpa would run into each other during these rest periods. When they did they could not help marveling at the irony of two Oconee boys meeting up in France.

After a five day rest, the II Corps was ordered back into the line near Montbrehan. By this time the British had advanced an additional three and three quarter miles, and was gearing up for a new offensive on October 8th. The "Old Hickory" boys would be back "in the thick of it" again. Between October 8th and 11th, the II Corps would participate with the British IV Army in a series of battles that would eventually bring them to the west bank of the Selle River. Two of those obscure fights are listed on Grandpa's discharge papers; Busigny and St. Souplet.

Busigny was a railroad town that had been under German occupation for the last four years. The 119th had the honor of capturing the town on October 8th, and according to the regimental history, liberated 1,800 French civilians. Before the enemy was completely driven out however, the grateful Frenchmen were in the streets offering the doughboys cups of hot coffee. The Frenchmen, it stated, "could not be too kind to their liberators." A great story and I wonder why Grandpa never spoke of it. The division continued its advance up through October 11th. Meeting little resistance, they managed to advance ten miles, and at 3: PM, October 9th, reached St. Souplet, on the west bank of the Selle River. At 5:30 the next morning the 30th attacked with the 119th and 120th regiments leading the attack. The 117th and 118th were held in reserve, while the British 25th and 6th Divisions attacked from the left and right flanks respectively. The 119th advanced

167

rapidly, with the 3rd Battalion (Grandpa's) experiencing a sharp fight in the local cemetery taking out those infernal machine guns. By noon, the town was firmly in possession of the 119th, and once again the streets were full of grateful Frenchmen greeting the Americans as their liberators.

Fighting resumed again on the eleventh, as an unsuccessful attempt was made to cross the heavily defended Selle River. In the course of the days fighting, a platoon from Grandpa's company K was nearly surrounded by the Germans. When the platoon commander asked for a volunteer to carry a message for reinforcements, Pvt. Robert Blackwell answered the call. Tragically, as he attempted to get through the heavy shell and machine gun fire, he was cut down. For his heroism and sacrifice Pvt. Blackwell would become yet another recipient of the Medal of Honor. I wondered, as I read Blackwell's citation, if Grandpa was in the surrounded platoon that day. Did he know Pvt. Blackwell?

As a result of the fighting from October 7th-11th, sixteen square miles were taken including Busigny, St. Souplet, and numerous other towns and farms. Over 2,000 French civilians were liberated and thousands of prisoners were taken, not to mention enemy material as well. Much had been accomplished and the men needed a rest. The 119th got one on the 11th and 12th, when they were billeted around the Van Le Prettre farm. A bath house formerly in possession of the Germans was found and promptly put to use. Grandpa should have gotten a good, hot shower that day.

Meanwhile, the German defenses on the eastern bank of the Selle, loomed large before the British and Americans. After a five day break the II Corps along with the British IV and French 1st armies, attacked across the river. In a heavy mist, the troops waded across the stream and attacked enemy trenches on the heights forcing the enemy back. On the 17th, after another hard fight, the 30th captured Molain and St. Martin-Riviere. They advanced another two miles and took Ribeauville on the 18th. On the 19th the division captured the village of Mazinqhien and faced another hard

168

fight east of town. "Every hedge sheltered enemy machine gun nests", wrote the divisional historians, "which with German trench mortars, poured murderous fire into our ranks". The attack was stymied, and while preparations were being made to re-new the attack, the division received orders to hold their ground. After covering five miles, and being in continuous combat for three straight days the men were exhausted. It had been a murderous two weeks. In their operations since October 5th, the 30th suffered over 4,000 casualties.

At 11:50 PM. October 19th, the 30th Division was mercifully relieved by the British 1st Division. Over the next few days, the weary doughboys trudged their way back over the same ground they had fought so hard over. Making their way through St. Souplet, Busigny and other towns they finally made it to Tincourt by October 22nd. The next day they got a ride taking a train to the Heill area. From there they marched to various towns and were billeted. Grandpa was stationed at Belincourt along with the rest of the 3rd Battalion.

Orville wrote that in late October or early November (which I believe places it during this march), that while marching back from the front, he became very weak. He told his commanding officer, who instructed him to fall out by the side of the road and wait for the medics. Later while Orville sat and waited, Grandpa marched by and saw him. Not realizing he was sick, he simply waved a greeting at his old friend. Eventfully medics did come by and Orville was taken to a hospital. When he was diagnosed with the flu, he was promptly quarantined in a shack behind the hospital, where he felt, he said, "terrible and all alone."

For the next three weeks the division busied itself with bathing and delousing, re-equipping, drilling, and generally preparing itself for re-entry into the line. Replacement's (mostly poorly trained, the divisional history noted) began to arrive the first week of November, and those who had recovered from their wounds rejoined their outfits. Grandpa remembered this period as a time of more maneuvers, marching, and drilling to stay in shape.

The conditioning maneuvers were designed to keep the men toughened up to the rain and cold, he explained. "We were mud all over much of the time from falling or climbing into shell holes", he told the *Vandalia Leader*. "We marched along the roads and had only bully beef and hard tack to eat. We rested ten minutes out of every hour. We had to keep tough because just loafing around lets a man get out of condition."

Time was also spent sightseeing. When they got the chance the soldiers would tour the many shattered towns, and villages left over from the German occupation. The city of Amiens was a popular spot, and according to *Borrowed Soldiers*, on November 2nd, members of the 30th attended a mass there for their fallen comrades. To the perceptive veteran all of the signs were there. The "Old Hickory" boys would soon be sent back to the front again. But little did they know that their war was over! For at the eleventh hour, on the eleventh day, of the eleventh month, an armistice was finally reached that ended the most deadly war in history up to that time.

Rumors of an armistice had been floating around a lot those last few day. "..There were always rumors going around, so you didn't know what to believe" Orville said. Nonetheless, on the morning of November 11th, Orville and the rest, accustomed as they were to the constant rumble of the big guns in the distance, heard something new that startled them that cool morning- *a deafening silence*! As dictated by the armistice, at 11: OO AM, the guns up and down the Western Front ceased firing. Moments later the air became filled with another sound as the joyful peal of the town's church bells announced the news. Orville, who was still recuperating in the hospital, was confused by the sudden silence and the tolling bells. Then somebody came in and excitedly told him, "that the war was really over!" Soon they would all be going home, and as Orville recalled, "what a wonderful feeling that was." Grandpa first heard the news while on one of those maneuvers. As Grandpa described to the *Vandalia Leader*, a horseman rode up and briefly spoke with an officer. Within minutes a bugler sounded the call to arms, and the men gathered to hear the great news. Naturally the scene erupted, as the men responded with "noise and helmets flying into the air!"

Now that the war was finally over, all the boys could think about was getting home, a task easier said than done. It would require a monumental effort– in a war of monumental efforts– to organize all of the logistics and transportation to get two million doughboys back to the U.S.A. For the 30th Division, it would be a nearly five month wait.

Chapter XVI

Coming Home!

April, 1918. A happy Corporal Rakers is finally back home.

On November 16th, the II Corps received field order # 23, informing them that they were being transferred from the British back to the A.E.F. They were no longer "borrowed soldiers." The divisions promptly returned all borrowed equipment to the British, and made preparations to re-locate to the Le Man's rest area. The movement began the next day, with various units boarding trains at Corbie. By the end of November, the entire division had been transferred to Le Mans and billeted throughout the region, with the 3rd Battalion at Beaumont Sur Sarthe.

With a wait of just under five months staring them in the face, the division realized they had to find ways to keep the men busy. Soldiers far from home, with too much time on their hands can spell trouble. The division's first impulse, naturally, was to continue drilling. Orville recalled that following his release from the hospital, time was spent marching and drilling, to "keep them occupied." However, on one occasion, Orville found another activity to keep himself "occupied". Like so many American soldiers, he wanted some war souvenirs. (There is an old saying that the British fight for their king, the French for glory, but Americans fight for souvenirs) So one day he ventured onto a nearby battlefield where the detritus of war still laid all about. There he collected a camouflaged German helmet, rifle, and cigarette lighter. Back in camp he put it all in a gunny sack and mailed it back home, "just for fun!" he said. Much to his amazement, when he arrived back in Oconee that spring, the sack with all its booty was sitting there waiting for him!

Predictably, the attempts to keep the men busy with more drilling and maneuvers was met with a less than enthusiastic response from the homesick veterans. The divisional history noted that it was very difficult to motivate the men to fight a, "hypothetical enemy on a mythological battle field..." when the very real experience of combat "was still fresh" in their minds. Not surprisingly, there were breaches of discipline. Apparently, these infractions became enough of a problem that on December 30th, the commanding General of the division, Brigadier General Samson

Fasion, issued what became known as the "New Year's Order." After wishing the men a happy New Years, he reminded them of General Pershing's post armistice dictum to not "engage in acts of lawlessness and rowdyism." Taking a more personal tack, he then told his disgruntled command how "dear" the division was to him, and how hard he had worked to build it. The "few isolated cases of lawlessness and rowdyism" had been very "distressing" to him. He then appealed to their pride by saying, "Are the men who broke the Hindenburg Line and drove the enemy twenty miles going to allow the glory and fame there achieved to be snatched from them by a few men devoid of pride and decency?" Then taking a firmer tone he ordered the men to turn in anybody whose acts would "bring the good name of the division into disrepute." In conclusion, he assured them the authorities would see to it that they were properly punished.

Appeals and threats were one way to deal with the discipline problems, but the division commanders knew that something else needed to be done. Starting in January, afternoon drill ceased, and athletic competition began. They proved to be very popular, and brought out a "keen rivalry" in the men. The division also organized competitive drills and inspections, with the goal of picking the best regiments from both the 30th and 27th Divisions. Then by a process of elimination they picked the best regiment overall. Unfortunately, for whatever reason-- as neither unit histories explained--the final stage of the competition never occurred. However, as far as the 30th was concerned, the 119th Infantry Regiment received the coveted honor of being declared the best in the entire division.

Over the course of the long wait to go home, three holidays came and went: Thanksgiving, Christmas, and New Year's. Regrettably, neither the divisional nor regimental histories made any mention of them. Perhaps there was nothing worth mentioning, but I would find that hard to believe. Wouldn't a special meal have been provided, some kind of decorations put up, or some kind of celebration taken place? Regardless, the histories are silent.

However, Grandpa did remember his Christmas in France. In the *Vandalia Leader* interview, he told of his Christmas dinner being brought to the men in a rolling kitchen. They were fed meat, a rare occasion at the front, and that it was "coarse and not too tasty." Probably horse steak he said, but he added "That brown gravy, was it ever good!"

In 1975, (I presume around Christmas) in a wonderful letter dictated to his daughter Joan, Grandpa shared even more details about his Christmas in France.

"Christmas day, 1918. I was in France. The war had just ended, so it was a good Christmas-that was all we could want.

We were staying in a little village in an old barn--about 12 of us. It was cold, four inches of snow on the ground, there was no heat and the wind blew through, so we hung gunny sacks over where the windows should have been.

We had to walk about as far as from our house in Ramsey to the little store to eat our meals, and for Christmas dinner we had meat-one of the only 2 or 3 times we had meat in France.

The meat was dark and strong, but it was hot and sure tasted good. (Interesting how this contradicts his comments in the Vandalia Leader) It must have been horse meat.

Later in the afternoon a buddy and I took a walk to the next village. We stopped at a house right beside the road and knocked. Two old ladies came to the door. They asked us in and we said 'vino, vino'- so they brought us a bottle and we sat there and drank it. Then we said 'encore' and they brought another bottle and we each had a glass and it was sour, so they laughed.

We paid them something and went back to our village."

A memorable Christmas indeed.

On January 21st, 1919, the division received a special guest. General Pershing, Commander of the A.E.F., made his second visit to the 30th Division. The division put on its best "bib and tucker" for the general and lined up for inspection. Later one of the general's staff officers made a rating of all the units in the division. The 119th was rated #1 in appearance, equipment, and marching in review. Yet another feather in the 119th's cap.

To the homesick Doughboys, the months of November, December, and January slowly passed by. Finally, during the first week of February the much anticipated, albeit slow, process of going home began. That week orders were given for the division to march to the forwarding camp on the outskirts of Le Mans. Here they would prepare themselves for the return trip with physical exams, equipment inspections, and of course delousing. By the middle of February, some units had received their certificates of clearance, and were ready to make the voyage home. The excitement surely was great, but a disappointment awaited them. Due to a change in destination from New York City to Charleston, South Carolina, there would be a delay in departure. They would have to wait a little longer.

Over a four- week period from March 17th to April 5th, nine transports would deliver the division across the Atlantic to Charleston (Two would sail to Newport News, Va.). For the 119th, its journey home began on February 11^{th,} with a march to the forwarding camps five kilometers (3.2 miles) away from Le Mans. After completing its preparations there, it left on March 12th and proceeded to the embarkation camp at St. Nazaire, arriving on the 13th and 14th. Here they stayed for the next three days, making their final preparations to go home.

It would take two ships to transport the 6000 men of the 119th and other units back home. On March 17th, various units set sail on the USS Madawaska. The rest of the regiment, which included Grandpa's, left four days later on the USS Huron. The trip home provided one more adventure for the 119th. Heavy winds and storms rocked both ships, prolonging the voyage even longer. I'm sure there were many a seasick doughboy on that stormy voyage, but whatever discomfort they felt would've been offset by the knowledge that at least there were no U-Boats stalking them this time.

After a thirteen day voyage, both ships finally arrived in Charleston on Wednesday, April 2nd. Naturally, the event created great excitement throughout the city, and was extensively covered by the local paper, *The News and Courier*. It reported that the Madawaska arrived first, at 8:30 AM, with 2, 485 men aboard. As it neared the lightship (a moored or anchored vessel with a beacon light to warn or guide ships at sea), a small flotilla of ships loaded with townsfolk, local dignitaries, and two bands, noisily sailed out to greet the vessel. With sirens and bands blaring, and whistles screeching, they met up as the Madawaska sailed past Fort Sumter, site of the opening shots of the Civil War, fifty- eight years earlier.

As the happy fleet circled the huge transport, cheers arose from the boats both large and small. To further welcome the Madawaska home, a seaplane swooped down low and dropped copies of *The News and Courier* on its decks. The papers, it was reported, were eagerly snatched up by the delighted soldiers. Meanwhile there was frantic activity on shore. Apparently the Madawaska had arrived sooner than expected. The paper noted that the Charleston Red Cross had to quickly make 3,000 sandwiches on short notice!

To reach the port terminal the transport had to sail eleven miles up the Cooper River. It was reported that as it got closer, and if the wind was blowing just right, the cheering of the expectant crowds waiting at the terminal could be heard downstream by the men. They, in turn, would return the cheers upstream with *"interest!"* The small, but noisy fleet continued to escort the Madawaska up river, eventually reaching the wharves, packed with cheering crowds. As the transport pulled in closer, cheer after cheer rose up from both the decks and wharves as doughboys, families, and neighbors traded greetings. At 11:00AM, the Madawaska finally docked and began to disembark its eager, khaki- clad cargo. Steady streams of soldiers, outfitted in all their gear and overseas caps, joyously poured down the gangplanks and

177

into the embracing crowd below. Red Cross workers moved amongst the doughboys handing out their hastily made sandwiches and cigarettes. A reporter for the *News and Courier* made his way to General Faison, looking for a quick interview, or a snappy quote. He got both. "We met the Germans" he quipped, *"and you know the result!"*

Very little time was spent on the wharves enjoying the crowd's warm adulation. There were trains to catch! Four or five trains (There is a discrepancy in the article) of roughly thirteen coaches and 650 men each, were loaded up. Their destination was Camp Jackson (Fittingly enough, considering their nickname), just outside Columbia S.C. Here, the 119th would be de-mobilized and begin the final leg home.

The Huron was late. The huge transport with its 3,122 anxious men, was due at noon, but would not arrive until much later in the day. The destroyer *USS Drayton* was the first to spot the lagging transport, which the paper described as "…a dim speck upon the horizon." Like reunited lovers, the two ships raced towards each other, and soon the figure of the Huron could be clearly seen: a large two-funnel, battleship gray, steamship. Once the *Drayton* reached the *Huron*, it circled the mighty ship. With the distinguished Citadel Cadet Band blaring martial airs, the crew and guests waved flags, and raised cheer after cheer. The *Drayton* and the rest of the flotilla, keeping at a safe distance, convoyed the Huron through the harbor, reaching Fort Sumter about 1:15.

Progress was slow. It was 4:30 before the *Huron* dropped anchor at quarantine to take on an inspecting officer. Oddly, the paper never mentioned the *Madawaska* being quarantined, and no explanation was given for the *Huron*. Clearly there was a concern about disease. Perhaps it was the flu, as the world was experiencing the worst influenza outbreak in history at the time. Meanwhile, while the *Huron* was being inspected, the men and crowds were entertained by two seaplanes swooping and diving overhead. One dropped several wreaths aboard the ship, welcoming the men home.

178

Debarking at the Port Terminals, Charleston, S.C.

It all must have seemed surreal to Grandpa. In the midst of the music and cheers, Grandpa looked back across the Atlantic and reflected on what he had been through. He had survived a great and terrible war that had consumed millions. He had seen and experienced more in fifteen months than most people do in a lifetime. Trench life, lousy food, lice, mud, blood, fatigue, fear, and death had robbed him of his innocence forever. He was no longer the naïve farm boy from small town Oconee. He was a veteran warrior now, who had been tested in so many ways and had survived. It's no wonder he would look back in disbelief, and ask himself, *"Did it really happen?"*

Finally at 5:50, the Huron weighed anchor, left the quarantine station, and headed further upstream to the Port Terminal. Here she would anchor and spend the night. At 8:00 the next morning, the men, who probably never wanted to see another boat again,

179

scrambled off the smelly, crowded transport. Like before, the Red Cross workers were waiting for them, and handed out sandwiches, soft drinks, papers, and cigarettes. At 9:30 the first troop train pulled out with the remaining five trains following at fifteen minute intervals. It wouldn't be long before they were bunking down in more comfortable quarters at Camp Jackson.

Throughout history victorious armies have come home, and proudly marched in parades, basking in their hard earned glory. The A.E.F. was no different, and its many divisions marched in parades throughout the land. For the various regiments of the 30th Division, parades took place in Memphis, Nashville, Chattanooga, and Knoxville, Tennessee; Winston-Salem and Raleigh, North Carolina and Columbia, South Carolina.

The 119th Regiment marched in its last parade in downtown Columbia, on Saturday, April 5th, 1919. According to the local paper *The Columbia Times,* the men journeyed to town in electric streetcars, arriving around noon. The parade wasn't scheduled to start until 4:00 PM, but even so, thousands of spectators had begun to pack the parade route, hours before its start. By parade time, the reviewing stand at Main and Hampton streets was overflowing with military and civilian dignitaries and their wives. General Samson L. Faison, the Governor, congressmen, and senators were all there to witness, and participate in the historic day. Colonel Metts' wife, young daughter, and father, J.I. Metts, were also on the stand. The senior Metts, or Captain Metts, as he was called during the Civil War, was a Confederate veteran of that war. He had served as Captain of the 3rd North Carolina Regiment, and was wounded at the Battle of Gettysburg. He currently was serving as commander of the North Carolina Division of Confederate Veterans. Now fifty- three years later, he would watch his son march with another victorious "Yankee" army.

With the air full of anticipation and excitement, the parade began on time as scheduled. Colonel Metts led the way, and as the *Times* proudly observed, not a single officer was on horseback. Just as they had led their men in France on foot, so too they would

180

also parade with them on foot! The men marched in platoon formation, wearing their helmets and cartridge belts. Arms were carried with fixed bayonets. Two military bands preceded the men, and when they reached Main Street, "The drum major of the regimental band swung his baton, the drum rattled, and the band sounded the opening airs of the matchless Southern air-*Dixie!*" The crowd, of course, roared its approval.

Ex-rebels on the reviewing stand? Bands playing Dixie? The Civil War may have been over for fifty three years, and Carolinians may have fought alongside New Yorkers, but clearly, here in Columbia S.C., the very cradle of secession, Southern pride and Confederate memories still ran deep.

The paper reported that the soldiers were a "fine looking lot" in their clean shoes and uniforms. They marched "splendidly" in lines straight "as a rule", and with their tread as steady as "clock ticks." When the crowds saw them, a cheer of "genuine admiration" broke out, up and down the street. When the marching doughboys reached the reviewing stand, Colonel Metts left and took his place with his family and other dignitaries. As each company passed by the stand, the officer would order *"EYES LEFT!"* Then, as each commanding officer brought his hand to a snappy salute, the eyes of the men "turned toward the sun." In one platoon, the *Times* reported, a 2nd Lt. saluted with his left hand, as his right had been badly wounded in battle. Bringing up the rear of the parade, was a decorated truck bearing a service flag with thirty-two stars. Above the flag were words honoring the memory of thirty two of Columbia's heroes who had made the ultimate sacrifice. "The parade of Saturday afternoon has not been equaled in majesty and splendor by any ever held here," the *Times* gushed. "The men say they have never been given a warmer reception,....unless it was last October 9th when they captured... St. Souplet."

The parade disbanded at Lady and Sumter Streets, where the men loaded their weapons on trucks. Now it was time to relax, and soak up all the Southern hospitality the city had to offer. The soldiers were "…guests of the people of Columbia," the *Times* announced, and were welcome to mingle with its citizens, and enjoy an evening of pleasure. Booths lined up and down Main Street provided refreshments. The men had their pick of candy, pies, cold drinks, sandwiches, chocolate, and homemade biscuits. After stuffing themselves, the men could attend any of the eight dances held that night in their honor. They had their choice of the Elks Club, the University gymnasium, or the Knights of Columbus, to name just a few. At midnight the fun ended, and then (the paper didn't say how) they made their way back to Camp Jackson. Here one more ritual awaited them the next day.

Sunday, April 6th, was the last time Grandpa and Orville would assemble as part of the 119th Infantry Regiment. At 3:30 that afternoon, the regiment was assembled in battalion formation on the camp parade ground. The first order of business that day was one last inspection by General Faison. Next came an award ceremony. With the regimental band playing, Colonel Metts led six honorees to the front of the regiment, to award them the Distinguished Service Cross. He then proceeded to read the citation for each man. With each citation, the Colonel described the individual's heroism, pinned a medal on his chest, and then warmly shook each man's hand. Afterwards, the six men took a position to the left of the General Faison, and watched as the regiment passed in review.

Following the ceremony, the regiment formed up in a rectangle with the General taking his place near the center. It would be the last time Faison would address the men. In a speech covered by the *Times*, he praised the spirit of the regiment. Despite the representation of many "climes" in a regiment dominated by Carolinians and Tennesseans, the spirit of the regiment, he said, was the "spirit of North Carolina and there is no greater spirit in the U.S.!" He praised their courage and battle performance. "There are," he boasted, *"no white feathers among you!"* He wished them well in civilian life, and assured them that they were better men for the experience. Then in closing, he hearkened back

182

to the Civil War, and quoted General Robert E. Lee, who once said, *"There goes North Carolinians. God bless them, they have always done their duty!"* With that, the band struck up a march and the regiment marched back to the barracks.

Eight days later, on April 14, Grandpa and Orville received their honorable discharges at Camp Grant, Illinois. What happened between the parade on the 6th and their discharge on the 14th, I can't say. Probably more paperwork and delays. In any case, the same day of their discharges, they boarded the Illinois Central at Rockford, and headed for home. According to Grandpa's discharge papers, he was coming home with his final army pay of $127.98. For some reason, Orville had less, with $103.94. Their discharge papers also listed what they were allowed to keep and take home, which was basically their uniform: overseas caps, leggings, poncho, overcoat, service coat, flannel shirts, shoes, stockings, undershirts, waist belt, gloves, collar discs, and a bronze victory button all made the list. Unfortunately, as far as Grandpa was concerned, none of that stuff survived. Moths, he once told me, saw to that. Who knows what happened to the collar discs and victory button. On the other hand, much of Orville's stuff, such as his helmet and gas mask, (neither of which, interesting enough, are listed on his discharge papers) did survive, and is currently in possession of his son, David Hinton.

It isn't clear when exactly Grandpa and Orville arrived home. It may have been the 14th or later. According to family lore Grandpa arrived in Pana about midnight. Older brother Henry and "others" (presumably family) were there waiting to pick him up and drive him home. Afterwards they stayed up late and drank beer. At some point, Mr. Warner, the banker who Grandpa had said goodbye to almost fifteen months earlier, came by. "You told me goodbye and I want to say hello," Mr. Warner reportedly said. The next day, or thereabouts, Grandpa posed for several photographs. He's dressed in his uniform, minus his service coat. He's wearing his overseas cap, flannel shirt, breeches and puttees. In one photo, he sits on a tree stump beside the barn. In an attempt to give him a more martial appearance, he quaintly holds the family shotgun. He's smiling, but he looks tired and thin. In another shot, he's laying prone- probably to humor his family-- and is aiming his shot gun at an invisible German in the distance.

Other than these few anecdotes and the photographs, there isn't much material to tell more about his homecoming, which is a shame. Nonetheless, I think we can assume certain things. Certainly his family and friends were thrilled to have him back home again. There most certainly would have been a period of adjustment (nightmares maybe?), as he settled back into civilian life. And certainly, there would have come the time, when his mother pulled him aside, and told him her miraculous story. That must've been a special moment for both. Tragically, their time together was brief, and probably weighted with joy and sorrow. Surely Grandpa knew, if not while away, then most certainly after he got back, that his mother was dying. In the end, Mary had gotten her dying wish. She got to see her son one more time before she died. It was another mother's prayer that God had answered. She died several months later, on July 1st, 1919.

In 1918, shortly before the St. Mihiel offensive, Lt. Hunter Wickersham wrote one of the most famous poems of World War I, *The Raindrops on Your Old Tin Hat*. It was written for mothers everywhere who suffered the agony of having a son away at war. When I read it, I could not help but to think of Mary Rakers.

Mary Rakers

The Raindrops on Your Old Tin Hat

The mist hangs low and quiet on a ragged line of hills,
There's a whispering of wind across the flat,
You'd be feeling kind of lonesome if it wasn't for one thing,
The patter of the raindrops on your old tin hat.

An' you just can't help a-figuring-sitting there alone-
About this war and hero stuff and that,
And you wonder if they haven't sort of got things twisted up,
While the rain keeps up its patter on your old tin hat.

When you step off with the outfit to do your little bit,
You're simply doing what you're s'posed to do-
And you don't take time to figure what you gain and lose—
It's the spirit of the game that brings you through.

But back at home she's waiting, writing cheerful little notes,
And every night she offers up a prayer,
And just keeps on a-hoping that her soldier boy is safe—
The mother of the boy who's over there.

And fellows, she's the hero of this great, big ugly war,
And her prayer is on the wind across the flat,
And don't you reckon it's her tears, and not the rain,
That's keeping up the patter on your old tin hat?

Chapter XVII
After The War

Third Annual Reunion
30th Division Veterans of Illinois
Belleville, Sept. 3, 1939
Grandpa is seated middle row, 4th from the left and Orville is seated
in the first row, 4th from the left.

Grandpa was twenty- two years old when he came home from France. He would live another seventy years. In time, as the years passed, he could put the war behind him, but never completely, as his stories will attest. Nonetheless, like most veterans, he got on with his life.

Initially he picked up where he left off before the war, and that was to continue to live and work on the Raker's farm. For a brief period, he ran a family restaurant situated along what is now Highway 51. Nine years later in 1928, he moved ten miles south to the town of Ramsey. He took up residence in a two-room house, and operated the family owned gas station that came with it. Here he would stay for the remaining sixty years of his life.

Orville, who had preceded Grandpa to Ramsey and worked in the bank, moved in with him. For the next eighteen months they lived the bachelor life, until one day Grandpa came home and announced "Orville, you gotta move out. I'm getting married!"

My grandmother, Katherine Marty, was the eldest child of Theodore and Maggie Marty, who raised their brood of nine children on a farm just south of Ramsey. Wanting more than what a farming life could offer, she traveled to Springfield IL., and enrolled at St. John's hospital to receive nurses' training. In 1924, she graduated at the top of her class with a nursing degree. Following graduation, Springfield became her home, as she pursued her profession at the hospital. Several years later, while visiting Ramsey, she met Grandpa on a blind date, and after a brief courtship, they married on June 5th, 1930. Between 1931 and 1944 they had five children: Joan, Mary Kay, my mother Mildred, George, and Elizabeth. What had been a two room house, quickly expanded, as more rooms, including an office fronting the house, were added to accommodate a growing family.

Grandpa supported his family, running the gas station and leasing nearby land to local farmers. They kept a cow for milk, raised chickens for the eggs, and kept a sheep for a pet. A large garden in the back provided them with potatoes, peas, green beans, tomatoes, onions, and beets. Besides the main house, there were several out- buildings such as a barn, chicken coop, wash house, and of course, the outhouse. They didn't have indoor plumbing until after the Second World War. When their work was done, there was a spacious north yard, with wonderful towering shade trees, to play and relax in.

During these years Grandpa and Orville kept in contact.

Orville worked at the Ramsey Bank until 1948 or so before resigning. It was said he was experiencing "nerve" problems and needed a rest. Probably Post traumatic stress syndrome, according to David Hinton, Orville's son. He eventually took on other jobs, such as working for the County Treasury office, secretary of the school board, and book keeper for a tractor business in Pana. In 1956, he and his wife moved to Amarillo, Texas to take another book- keeping job. By 1966 he was in poor health. He decided to resign and move back to Ramsey once again. Here he and his wife would live for the rest of their days. In 1987 Orville died from an aneurism.

At some point, Grandpa joined the American Legion. Formed immediately after the war in 1919, its mission was to organize commemorative events, and lobby the government on behalf of veteran interests. Wearing their distinctive blue overseas caps, he, Orville, and other veterans would serve as honor guards at veteran funerals and Memorial Day ceremonies. He marched in his share of parades, and starting in the late thirties, attended veteran reunions. Held in places like Vandalia, Ramsey, Belleville, and Pana, they were attended by Illinois "Old Hickory" veterans. These reunions were instructive for Grandma, and probably the other wives as well. Grandpa didn't talk much about the war at home, but he did at the reunions. I remember Grandma saying how she would overhear the men talking about their lost buddies. They would pose for group photos, just like they did that cold morning on the Shelbyville Courthouse steps, two decades earlier. On September 3rd, 1939, their third annual reunion took place in Belleville. Not a big deal really, except two days earlier, World War II started with Germany's invasion of Poland. That pretty much put an end to Wilson's goal of fighting a "War to end all wars." Believe it or not, the outbreak of the Second World War came as a shock to Orville and Grandpa, as neither could believe that another war could break out so quickly. Both were extremely disappointed that the war they had fought so hard in, didn't fulfill its lofty goal.

Over the years, their children grew up, moved away, got married and had families of their own. Many a time, my folks would stuff my four siblings and me into the station wagon, head east on I-70, and make the six- hour trek to Ramsey. Grandma would fry chicken and bake rhubarb pie. We kids would play in, and get lost in the north corn field. It was a sure bet one of us would annoy the adults, banging on the piano. I can still hear, and *feel,* the low, heavy, rumble of the Illinois Central passing by on the tracks behind the house. Probably a double header. I can also still hear the service bell ringing, as a car pulled into the station for gas. Didn't matter if it was dinner time or not, Grandpa always jumped up and hurried out to wait on a customer. And of course, there were the stories. Funny how you take it all for granted; then one day it's gone.

In 1978, after fifty years of pumping gas, Grandpa retired. Being a practical man, Grandpa had the front office torn out. Being far more sentimental, I was sorry to see it go, with its pop machine and candy counter. I considered it a good day if Grandpa let me have a bottle of orange pop. The gas station and Grandpa were a bit of an institution in Ramsey, and his retirement was the subject for several newspaper stories.

In 1980 Grandpa and Grandma celebrated their fiftieth wedding anniversary. All of their children and grandchildren converged upon Ramsey for several days of visiting, eating, and playing, as we celebrated their golden anniversary. In the photograph you can see them positively glowing with joy and pride. Over the next eight years, they filled their time following the same routines as they always had. It was during these years I would make my summer visits. From time to time, he and Orville would get together and discuss old times. I can remember Orville sadly recalling the war saying, "We lost so many boys George, we lost so many boys." as Grandpa, tightlipped, would listen in silence. In time my grandparents became increasingly feeble. Grandpa's vision and hearing declined, and Grandma steadily lost her memory, but fortunately they were able to stay in their home until the end, compensating for each other's weaknesses.

On March 30th, 1988, Grandpa took a terrible fall. The water softener man was in the kitchen cellar doing his job, when Grandpa, apparently not seeing the opening in the floor, took a step and tumbled into the gaping hole. He sustained a severe concussion, and was taken at once to St. John's Hospital in Springfield. The family was immediately summoned. When I arrived a day or two later, my Aunt Joan was sitting with him in his room. He was unconscious, but she tried to tell him I was there. Somehow, he slowly sat up and uttered my name. Then with a groan, he collapsed back into his bed, unconscious.

My name, were the last words I ever heard him say.

Grandpa died on April 18th, 1988. He was ninety- two years old. Grandma passed away on May 18th, exactly one month later. Both are buried side- by- side in the Catholic Cemetery outside of town. At Grandpa's funeral, an honor guard from the American Legion was there to honor one of its own. Following the service, a bugler played Taps. As its mournful melody drifted across the Illinois prairie, tears streamed down my face. Next to his stone is a simple marker. For those who take the time to stop and look, it tells them that a veteran, a *doughboy*, lies in peace there.

Two 'Old Hickory" boys sharing memories about the armistice sixty-six years later. Veterans Day, Nov. 11, 1983.   Grandpa and Orville remained friends for a lifetime.

At the time of Grandpa's death, there weren't many doughboys left. The last of them, Frank Buckles, passed away at the age of 110 on February 27th, 2011. Both at one time had been part of a mighty, four million man army that today only exists in our memories and the history books. In many ways, Grandpa's war was universal. Like soldiers of any war, he knew hunger, fear, and fatigue. But his experiences were also unique, with stories full of humor, sadness, rebellion, disgust, grief, and faith. Growing up, I was privileged to hear his wonderful stories. It has been my honor to save them.

The "Bought Uniform" Story

There is a photograph of Grandpa that is a popular one in the family, and is displayed in most of our homes. It shows him wearing his uniform looking quite handsome. The story surrounding the photograph was that on a brief stop in Chicago during his trip home, Grandpa bought a new uniform for $23 or so, and posed for his picture in a local studio. For years we accepted that story without question. But as I researched my book, certain details – or lack of them – began to bother me.

It started with the lack of collar discs and any insignia on his uniform. It kept pestering me. Why were they missing? Collar discs by the way, were one inch bronze discs that were worn on the collar of the uniform. One disc had the letters US stamped on it, and the other would have a symbol for the branch of service the soldier served in, i.e. crossed rifles for infantry. According to his discharge papers he had collar discs, and as a corporal he would have had stripes to show his rank. Not only that, he would've also had a gold stripe on his lower left sleeve to indicate six months war service, and a division patch on his left shoulder. By contrast, in Orville's photo he is wearing the patch. Wouldn't Grandpa be proud of this and want to be seen wearing it? Besides, Regulations would have required it.

Another thing that bothered me was the idea Grandpa would buy a new uniform. It defies logic, and I don't think it's consistent with Grandpa's character. He already had a uniform and I just can't see Grandpa, who was a thrifty and practical man, spending 15 percent of his army take home pay on a uniform, when he already had a perfectly good one. Another detail, which I would have overlooked, if not for the help of well known WWI authority Mark Beveridge, was the shirt Grandpa is wearing. It's white. Only officers wore white shirts: Enlisted men wore Olive drab flannel shirts. To do so otherwise was against army regulations. Grandpa was a bit of a rebel, but I seriously doubt he would have gone that far.

Lending further evidence that the oft told story is bogus, is another photograph Aunt Agnes gave me. When I looked at it closely, I noticed that the background images where identical to the background in the photo in question. Clearly the photos had been taken at the same time. In this picture Grandpa is standing and we get a full view of his uniform. He is wearing canvas leggings, the likes of which he would have worn *before* going overseas. Now, in and of itself this would not be decisive evidence. After all, if he bought a new uniform, would it not come with the leggings? But in the barnyard photograph, that we do know was taken when he returned, he is wearing the wool puttees he would have worn in France, as well as a wool olive drab shirt. *If he had a new uniform why isn't he wearing it for the family photos?*

Clearly the story surrounding this photo is false. Unlike the other photographs included in this book we lack the true story behind it. The question becomes then, when was this picture taken and where? All I can do is speculate.

I believe that Grandpa posed for this photo *before* he left for

France. It is possible it was taken in Pana, or Shelbyville perhaps. It was not uncommon for studios to provide uniforms to their clients to have their picture taken before going off to the army, providing a keepsake to give to the folks back home. I found a newspaper ad in the Shelbyville *Daily Union* that advertised a commemorative book it was sponsoring after the war. It encouraged all Shelby County veterans to have their picture taken for the book. And in case they needed it, *a uniform could be provided by Ackenhead Studios*. The same studio by the way, that took all of those photographs of the contingents before they went off to training camp. No doubt these uniforms would have been basic affairs, lacking any descriptive details such as insignia and so forth, which would explain the lack of these details in Grandpa's picture. So it's possible he had the photo taken there. It's also possible he had it taken at a local studio at Camp Taylor or Camp Sevier. A quick perusal of the original photograph would easily solve this mystery, but unfortunately no name of the photographer is on it. I believe that in all likelihood, Grandpa went to a studio in one of those three places and wore a borrowed uniform to have a photo taken to give to his family.

How the "bought uniform" story ever got started I'll never know. Alas my dear readers, such is history!

Epilogue

Between July and October 1918, the 30th Division lost 1,641 officers and men killed, 6, 774 wounded, 198 missing, and 27 were taken prisoner, for a total of 8,415 casualties. Twelve men received the Medal of Honor-- four of them posthumously-- the highest of any Division in the A.E.F. Three hundred and twenty one received the Distinguished Service Cross and another fourteen received the Distinguished Service Medal. There were so many decorated heroes in the division, it took sixty pages to list them all in the divisional history.

Shortly after the Battle of Bellicourt, a temporary American cemetery was put in place just a half mile from the village of Bony. Here were buried the men of the 27th and 30th Divisions who lost their lives that bloody September day. In time it was decided to make the cemetery permanent, and today it is known as the Somme American Cemetery. Eventually men from other campaigns were buried here as well, and today the cemetery contains the graves of 1,833 Doughboys. Three Medal of Honor recipients lie in peace here, including Pvt. Robert Blackwell of Grandpa's Company K.

The cemetery is surrounded by a low stone wall decorated with roses, trees, and vines. The headstones are separated into four plots by paths that intersect at a flagpole; there an American flag flaps in the wind. The longer path leads you to a chapel at the eastern end of the cemetery where a massive bronze door greets you. Carved above it are the words "For Those Who Died for Their Country". As you enter, you see an altar with a cross-shaped window of crystal glass hanging above it. A soft light flows through the window, creating a feeling of reverence and respect. Further light is provided by side windows with displays of Corps and divisions insignias. On the walls are carved the names of the men who lost their lives, and flanking the altar, and hanging over the entrance, are American flags. Outside the chapel, standing guard above it all, are two carved American eagles.

The Somme American Cemetery
Photograph by American Battle Monument Commission.

Three miles away, and built directly over the St. Quentin Canal tunnel, is a massive monument of white marble dedicated to all American units who served with the British during the war. Built by the U.S. Government, the monument consists of a sculpted American eagle, flanked by two allegorical figures representing Victory and Remembrance. On raised letters, and on a gilded background is carved a dedicatory inscription. Inscribed on a frieze below, are the names of the battles the American units fought in. Proudly carved into the wall of the monument, are the insignias of the 27th and 30th Divisions. On the rear of the monument is a map illustrating the operations that took place in the area, and a nearby terrace provides the visitor a commanding view of the battlefields the 27th and 30th Divisions fought over.

Acknowledgments

While it's my name that's on the cover of this book, there were many other people who helped me immensely in the completion of the project. I must start with the kind and helpful (Is there any other kind?) librarians of the Shelbyville Pubic Library. They were the ones who directed me to their microfilm collection that proved to be such a boon to my research. Many thanks to those fine ladies. My thanks also to the librarians of the Richland County Public Library in Columbia, South Carolina, and the Charleston Public Library in Charleston, South Carolina. They patiently took my numerous phone calls and answered my questions. Their diligence in tracking down, and making copies of the newspaper articles I needed is greatly appreciated.

The research and curator staff at the National World War I Museum and Liberty Memorial here in Kansas City, were of tremendous value in my research. Many thanks to archivist Jonathan Casey, who answered my questions and helped direct my research in their outstanding research room. (If I may boast, I was the first one to use the room shortly after the renovated museum opened in 2006!) I owe special thanks to curator Doran Cart, who took time from his busy schedule to meet with me, and patiently analyze some of my photographs. Speaking of photographs, I owe a debt of gratitude to Mark Beveridge, Museum registrar at the Truman Presidential Library and well known World War I authority, for his assistance in also helping me analyze one of Grandpa's photographs. I must also express my gratitude for the archivist whose name, I much regret, I've long since forgotten. She worked at the museum the summer of 1988 when I first began my research. It was she who taught me how to preserve old documents, and first showed me a copy of the Divisional History that aided me so much in my writing. Thank you, whoever you are!

I also want to thank historian and the Investigative Archivist at the National Archives, Mitchell Yockelson. The timely publication of his book *Borrowed Soldiers* was of tremendous

201

help, providing important answers to some of my most nagging questions. Mr. Yockelson was very generous with his time and resources, answering my E-Mail queries, contributing the Foreword, and allowing me the use of a map from his book.

I feel like I must also thank those people who were willing to listen to this novice writer read his rough drafts aloud, and offer feedback and encouragement. Special thanks to my daughter Hannah, retired Ohio State History Professor, Ray Muessig and his wife, LaVonne, my good friend Mike Sievers, JoAnn Turkett, and of course my mom. I especially want to thank my wife Laura who not only listened to me read, but also provided invaluable technical assistance on the computer.

Finally, I must extend my sincere gratitude to Debra Stevenson, who was willing to serve as my editor and proofreader. No small job given her hectic schedule. Thank you for cleaning up my many mistakes. I only hope, I have made sufficient and proper use of commas, dashes, hyphens, colons, and semi-colons to please you.

Bibliography

Primary Sources

Metts, Colonel John B.; *Something of the Operations of the 119th Infantry, A Brief History of the 119th Infantry Regiment, 30th Division*

Walker, Major John O.; Graham, Major William; Fauntleroy, Captain Thomas; *Official History of the 120th Infantry, "3rd North Carolina" 30th Division, From August 5, 1917 to April 17, 1919, Canal Sector-Ypres-Lys Offensive, Somme Offensive*

Shelbyville Daily Union. April 3rd, February 21st, February 22nd, February 23rd, March 30th, September 28th, November 7th, 1918

Shelbyville Daily Democrat. February 21st, February 22nd, February 23rd, February 26th, February 28, March 7, March 30, April 4th, April 13,1918

The News and Courier (Charleston, South Carolina). April 3rd, 1919

The State (Columbia, South Carolina) April 6th, 1919

Columbia Record (Columbia, South Carolina) April 5th, April 6th, 1919

Vandalia Leader. November, 1976

Ramsey News Journal. 1979

Hinton, Orville. *World War I Remembered*. Date unknown

Rakers, John George. Christmas Letter, Winter, 1975

Rakers, John George. Discharge Papers, April 14th, 1919

Hinton, Orville. Discharge Papers, April 14th, 1919

Rakers, John, Discharge Papers, 1919

Hinton, Orville. *World War I Remembered*. Date unknown

Interviews

Rakers, George; summer 1985

Rakers, Agnes; July 12th and July 15, 1988

Rakers, John; July 17, 1988

Hinton, David. Video interview with George Rakers and Orville Hinton. Early Seventies

Hinton, David. Interview. August 18, 2013

Secondary Sources

Murphy, Elmer A.; Thomas, Robert S. *The Thirtieth Division in the World War; Old Hickory*. The Old Hickory Publishing Group,

Lepanto, Arkansas. 1936

Conway, Coleman Berkley. *History, 119th Infantry, 60th Brigade, 30th Division, U.S.A. Operations in Belgium and France. 1917-1919.* Published by the Wilmington Chamber of Commerce, North Carolina. 1920

Shelby County Historians, Davis, Leslie D. Editor in Chief. *Shelby\ County in the World War.* 1919

Yockelson, Mitchell A.; *Borrowed Soldiers, American's under British Command, 1918.* University of Oklahoma Press. 2008

Laskin, David; *The Long Way Home, An American Journey From Ellis Island to the Great War.* Harpers Collins Publishers. 2010

Groom, Winston; A Storm in Flanders, the Ypres Salient, 1914-1918, Tragedy and Triumph on the Western Front. Grove Press, New York. 2002

Stallings, Lawrence; Wyeth, M.S. *The Story of the Doughboys, the A.E.F. in World War I.* Harpers and Row Publishers. 1963

Morrin, Albert; *The Yanks Are Coming, The United States in the First World War.* Macmillan Publishing Company. 1986

Bosco, Peter; Bowman, John. *America at War. World War I.* Maple-Vail Book Manufacturing Group. 1991

Forty, Simon; *World War I, A Visual Encyclopedia.* PRC Publishers Ltd. 2002

Winter, Jay; Baggett, Blaine. *The Great War and the Shaping of the 20th Century.* Penguin Group. 1996

Haythornthwaite, Philip J. *The World War One Source Book.* Brockhampton Press London. 1992

Urwin, Gregory J.W.; *The United States Infantry; An Illustrated History 1775-1918.* Sterling Publishing Co. Inc. New York. 1991

Toland, John; *No Man's Land.* Doubleday and Company, Inc. Gordon City, New York. 1980

Jantzen, Steven; *Hooray For Peace, Hurrah For War; The United States in World War I.* Alfred A. Knopf, Inc. 1971

Gawne, Jonathan; *Over There! The American Soldier in World War I* . Greenhill Books. 1997

Eisenhower, John S.D.; *Yanks, the Epic Story of the American Army in World War I.* The Free Press. 2001

Mead, Gary; *The Doughboys, America and the First World War.* The Overlook Press. 2000

Prior, Robin; Wilson, Trevor; *The First World War*. Cassell Publishing. 1999

Zieger, Robert H.; *America's Great War, World War I and the American Experience*. Bowman and Littlefield Publishing Inc. 2000

Farwell, Byron; *Over There, the United States in the Great War, 1917-1918*. W.W. Norton and Company Inc. 1999

Goldstein, Donald M; Maihafer, Harry J.; *America in World War I*. Brassey's Inc. 2004

Coffman, Edward M. *The War to End All Wars, The American Military Experience in World War* I The University of Wisconsin Press. 1968

American Armies and Battlefields in Europe. U.S. Government Printing. 1938

Laffin, John; *A Western Front Companion1914-1918, A-Z source to the Battles, Weapons, People, Places, and Combat* Alan Sutton Publishing Limited. 1994

Pope, Stephen; Wheat, Elizabeth Anne; Robbins, Professor Keith, Consultant Editor. *The Dictionary of the First World War.* St. Martin's Press, New York. 1995

Lemmon, Dr. Sarah McCulloh; Midgette, Nancy Smith; *North Carolina's Role in the First World War.* North Carolina Office of Archives and History. 2013

Griess, Thomas E.; Atlas of the Great War. Avery Publishing Group, Wayne New Jersey. 1986

The Internet

The Doughboy Center. Http://www. WorldWarI.com

The Patriot Files. www.patriot files.com

http:// www.history.com/This day in history/ allied forces break through the Hindenburg Line

http:// en.wikipedia.org/wiki/Hindenburg Line

http:// www. Historyofwar.org/articles/battles_Cambrai_St.Quinten.html

http:// en.wikipedia.org/wiki/Battle of St. Quinten Canal

http://statelibrary.dcr.state.nc.us/WWI/30th ops.htm

http://en.wikipedia.org/w.index.barrage (artillery)

Illustration Credits

Unless otherwise noted Photos and illustrations are from the personal files of Mark Armato, or *The Thirtieth Division in the World War; Old Hickory*

Village of Bellicourt and St. Quentin Canal; U.S. Army Signal Corps
SC-28404 RG 111 NARA October 10th, 1918

New York Headline; Col. Red Reeder, *The Story of the First World War*
Duel, Sloan and Pearce. 1962

Uncle Sam; James Montgomery Flagg, 1917

30th Division Patch
Wikepedia.org/wiki/Division_insignia_of_the_United_States_Ar my

Map/ Ypres Salient; *commonwealth war graves commission site*
www.cwgc.org/ypres.default.asp

Map/ Hindenburg Line; Col. Red Reeder *The Story of the First World War* Duell, Sloan, and Pearce. 1962

Map/ Battle of Bellicourt; Mitchell Yockelson *Borrowed Soldiers*
University of Oklahoma Press. 2008

Somme Cemetery: American Battle Monument Commission

Doughboy illustration; *Prudential Army-Navy Booklet World War 1 copyright 1917*

National World War I Museum, Kansas City, Missouri, USA

The author...

Before retiring Mark Armato taught American History in the North Kansas City School District for thirty-two years. When he wasn't teaching he spent his time hosting workshops on teaching history, re-enacting, and performing as historical characters for a variety of audiences. He has been married to his lovely wife Laura for twenty-four years, has four great kids, and a dog named Fred, with a Napoleon complex. In his spare time Mark likes to read, write, travel, play guitar, wood work, hang out in book stores, and browse thrift shops looking for that perfect deal.

The author, wearing Orville Hinton's 'Tin Hat.'